PM photo by Haberman

Babe and the kids.

BABE RUTH

The Big Moments of The Big Fellow

TOM MEANY

A. S. Barnes and Company . . . New York

1958

TO EDWARD GRANT BARROW

Who helped Babe Ruth help baseball

Preface

This book is by no means intended to be a biography of Babe Ruth. It isn't even Ruth's "own" story, as those ghost-written autobiographies are so often termed. It is merely one man's impressions of the greatest baseball figure who ever lived, an attempt to reflect a few of the many colorful facets that make up this fabulous character.

Ruth was an established star by the time I coverd the 1923 World Series, my first actual contact with him, although I had played hookey from school to see him play ball before that. I was with the Yankees on each of their spring training trips from 1924, either for all or part of the training period, and covered all the subsequent World Series. Through a quirk of the schedule, I happened to be in Boston on June 2, 1935, when Babe quit the Braves, his last appearance as a major league player. Thus, my own activity as a sports writer closely paralleled the greater part of Ruth's career, and I was privileged to get to know him intimately both as baseball idol and man.

For Ruth's early background I am indebted to many baseball figures no longer with us—to Uncle Wilbert Robinson, who had been his host at the Georgia hunting lodge of Dover Hall; to Cap Huston, original partner of Colonel Ruppert in the purchase of the Yankees; to Bill Slocum and Sid Mercer, two of the finest sports writers and gentlemen who ever traveled with the Yankees or with any ball club, for that matter; to Miller Huggins, who made the first serious study of that complex personality known as Ruth; to Mark Roth, for many years Yankee road secretary; to Joe Kelley, one of the original old Orioles, who volunteered to act, briefly, as Ruth's chaperon; to Chick Fewster, a teammate of Ruth's; to Eddie Bennett, Yankee batboy; to Charley O'Leary, Yankee coach, and to many, many others.

While preparing this material, I had occasion to consult with Edward Grant Barrow, who knew Ruth better perhaps than anybody else; with Joe Engel, who saw Ruth pitching for the Baltimore "home"; with Tom Sheehan, one of Babe's early cronies on the Yankees; with Mel Webb, sports writer for the Boston *Globe,* who was covering the Red Sox when Ruth was first purchased; with Duffy Lewis, road secretary of the Boston Braves and a teammate of Ruth's on the Red Sox; with Arthur Mann, Dodger official who was a baseball writer for the New York *Evening World,* covering the Yankees when Babe hit his sixty home runs; Jim Kahn, New York *Sun,* and Daniel M. Daniel, New York *World-Telegram.*

Of incalculable value were the writings of Fred Lieb, baseball author and authority, who writes weekly for *The Sporting News,* and the advice of Christy Walsh, Ruth's business manager since 1921.

This story, then, if such it may be called, is the result of a combination of circumstances, of personal experiences, of something read here, of something heard there; of nearly a quarter of a century of covering sports, no small part of which was spent sitting up nights and talking about the "big fellow."

To those whom I have mentioned as being of assistance to me, my deepest thanks.

To those whom I should have mentioned as being of assistance to me, and didn't, my humblest apologies.

TOM MEANY

Foreword

I'm glad that Tom Meany has written a book about Babe Ruth. Like many other newspapermen, but especially the baseball writers who traveled with the Yankees, Tom Meany did much to publicize and dramatize Babe's feats both on and off the ballfield and it is fitting and proper that he should eventually put his recordings and recollections into a book.

For the greater part of Babe Ruth's active career from 1921 on, I managed Babe's many business activities, throwing me in close and constant contact with the big fellow and giving me an opportunity to know him differently and better than all but an intimate few.

Babe Ruth contributed more to baseball than his home runs and more to sports than his tremendous personal popularity. It is entirely possible that a ball player will come along who will hit more than 60 home runs in a single season, as the Babe did in 1927, but it is extremely doubtful that there ever will be a ball player, or any athlete, who ever again will capture the imagination and heart of the American public on the same grand scale that Ruth did.

I've known the author, Tom Meany, a good many years, ever since he first went to work on the old New York Telegram under Joe Williams. In fact, I hired him on my staff of ghost writers for the 1936 World Series and found when the Series opened that he had sublet the assignment, the only ghost writer I ever employed who had a ghost writer of his own! Tom, of course, traveled frequently with the Yankees when Ruth was an active player and always seemed to me to have a sympathetic understanding of the Babe. In line with that last, I might mention that when Babe, after quitting the Braves in 1935, played an exhibition game with some semi-pros at Dyckman Oval in the Bronx, I found Meany up there in the press box, scoring the game as industriously as though it were a World Series contest.

My association with Babe Ruth through twenty years, though often turbulent, was never unpleasant and certainly never dull. I only hope that through the medium of this book more people gain an appreciation of the tremendous imprint he has left on the national pastime, on its play and its pay, its strategies and its salaries. He was more than the greatest home run hitter in baseball history. In my opinion, Babe Ruth was the greatest single influence on sports of the century.

CHRISTY WALSH

Ruth's Complete Record

BABE RUTH'S RECORDS

American League

Most runs, season—177; Yankees, 152 games, 1927.

Most years leading league in runs—8; Red Sox, 1919; Yankees, 1921-2-3-4-6-7-8. (*)

Most runs batted in, lifetime—2209. (*)

Most years leading league runs batted in—6; Red Sox, 1919; Yankees, 1920-21-23-26-28. (*)

Most years 100 or more runs batted in—13; Red Sox, 1919; Yankees, 1920-21-23-24-26-27-28-29-30-31-32-33. (Tied with Lou Gehrig, Jimmy Foxx.) (*)

Most years leading league in long hits—7; Red Sox, 1918-19; Yankees, 1920-21-23-24-28. (**)

Most long hits, lifetime—1356 (506-2b; 136-3b; 714-hr). (*)

Most long hits, season—119 (44-2b; 16-3b; 59-hr) Yankees, 1921. (*)

Most years leading league in extra bases on long hits—9; Red Sox, 1918-19; Yankees, 1920-21-23-24-26-28-29. (*)

Most years 100 or more extra bases on long hits—14; Red Sox, 1919; Yankees, 1920-21-22-23-24-26-27-28-29-30-31-32-33. (***)

Most years 200 or more extra bases on long hits—4; Yankees, 1920-21-27-28. (*)

Most extra bases on long hits, lifetime—2920. (*)

Most extra bases on long hits, season—253; Yankees, 1921. (*)

Most total bases, season—457, Yankees, 1921. (*)

Highest slugging percentage, lifetime—.690. (*)

Most home runs, 5 consecutive games—7; June 10-14, 1921; Yankees. (****)

Most home runs, bases filled, season—4; Red Sox, 1919. (*****)

Most home runs, bases filled, consecutive games—Twice; Yankees, Sept. 27-29, 1927; Yankees, Aug. 6-7, 1929. (*)

Most home runs, season—60; Yankees, 1927. (*)

Most home runs, lifetime—714. (*)

Most years leading league in home runs—12; Red Sox, 1918 (tied with C. Walker); 1919; Yankees, 1920-21-23-24-26-27-28-29-30-31 (tied with L. Gehrig) . (*)

Most years 50 or more home runs—4; Yankees, 1920-21-27-28. (*)

Most years 40 or more home runs—11; Yankees, 1920-21-23-24-26-27-28-29-30-31-32. (*)

Most years 30 or more home runs—13; Yankees, 1920-21-22-23-24-26-27-28-29-30-31-32-33. (*)

Most home runs two consecutive seasons—114; Yankees, 60—1927, 54—1928. (*)

Most times two or more home runs, one game, lifetime—72. (*)

Most bases on balls, lifetime—2056. (*)

Most years leading league, bases on balls—11; Yankees, 1920-21-23-24-26-27-28-30-31-32-33. (*)

Most consecutive years leading league, bases on balls—4; Yankees, 1930-31-32-33. (*)

Most years 100 or more bases on balls—13. (*)

Most consecutive years 100 or more bases on balls—5; Yankees, 1930-34. (*-A)

Most bases on balls, season—170; Yankees, 1923, 152 games. (*)

Most strikeouts, lifetime—1330. (*)

(*) —also major league record
(**) —tied with Hans Wagner for major league record
(***) —tied with Lou Gehrig for major league record
(****) —tied with Jim Bottomley for major league record
(*****) —tied with Wildfire Schulte, Lou Gehrig, Rudy York and Vince DiMaggio for major league record
(*-A) —tied with Max Bishop, Harland Clift and Charley Keller for American League record

World Series

Most series played—10; Red Sox, 1915-16-18; Yankees, 1921-22-23-26-27-28-32.

Most times playing on winning club—7. (*)

Most series hitting .300 or better—6; Yankees, 1921-23-26-27-28-32.

Highest batting percentage, four or more games, one series—.625; Yankees, 1928, four games.

Most runs; total series—37.

Most runs, one series—9; Yankees, 1928. (**)

Most consecutive games, one or more runs, one or more series—9; Yankees, 2, 1927; 4, 1928; 3, 1932.

Most base hits, one series—10; Yankees, 1928, four games.

Making one or more base hits in each game, one series—3; Yankees, 1923, six games; 1928, 1932, four games.

Most two-base hits, one series—3; Yankees, 1928, four games. (***)

Most home runs, total series—15.

Most home runs, one series—3; Yankees, 1923, six games; 4, Yankees, 1926, seven games.

Most home runs, game—3; Yankees, 1926 and 1928.

Making two home runs in a game—Twice; 1923, 1932. (****)

Most total bases, total series—96.

Most total bases, one series—22; Yankees, 1928, four games; 19, Yankees, 1923, six games.

Most total bases, game—12; Yankees, 1926 and 1928.

Most long hits, one series—6; Yankees, 1928, four games; 5, Yankees, 1923, six games.

Most long hits, total series—22.

Most extra bases on long hits, total series—54.

Most extra bases on long hits, game—9 (twice) ; Yankees, 1926, 1928.

Most bases on balls, total series—33.

Most bases on balls, one series—8; Yankees, 1923, six games; 11, Yankees, 1926, seven games.

Most bases on balls, game—4. (*****)

Most strikeouts, total series—30.

Most series hitting .300 or better—6.

Pitcher winning longest game—Ruth, 14 innings, Red Sox vs. Dodgers, 1916.

Most consecutive innings pitched, no runs, total series—Ruth, 29-2/3.

(*) —Bill Dickey was on the winning club eight times, but did not play in 1928 series, although eligible. Lou Gehrig was on the winning club seven times, but did not play in the 1939 series, although eligible
(**)—tied with Lou Gehrig
(***) —tied with Hank Gowdy
(****) —tied by several players
(*****) —tied with Fred Clarke, Dick Hoblitzel

RECAPITULATION

Babe Ruth holds or shares a total of 61 baseball records, of which 28 are World Series records. Of these, he holds 23 outright. In league play, Ruth set 33 records, of which 27 are major league records, the others American League records. Of these major league records Ruth holds 22 by himself.

Courtesy The Little Red Book, Al Munro Elias Bureau, N. Y. C.

RUTH, GEORGE HERMAN (BABE)

Born, Baltimore, Md., February 6, 1895
Bats Left. Throws Left. Height 6 feet, 2 inches. Weight, 220 pounds

Year	Club	Lea.	Pos.	G.	A.B.	R.	H.	S.B.	Avg.
1914	Balt.-Providence a	I.L.	P-OF	46	121	22	28	4	.231
1914	Boston b	A.L.	P	5	10	1	2	0	.200
1915	Boston	A.L.	P-OF	42	92	16	29	0	.315
1916	Boston	A.L.	P-OF	67	136	18	37	0	.272
1917	Boston	A.L.	P-OF	52	123	14	40	0	.325
1918	Boston	A.L.	P-OF	95	317	50	95	6	.300
1919	Boston c	A.L.	P-1B-OF	130	432	103	139	7	.322
1920	New York	A.L.	1B-OF	142	458	158	172	14	.376
1921	New York	A.L.	OF-1B	152	540	177	204	17	.378
1922	New York	A.L.	OF	110	406	94	128	2	.315
1923	New York	A.L.	OF	152	522	151	205	17	.393
1924	New York	A.L.	OF	153	529	143	200	9	.378
1925	New York	A.L.	OF	98	359	61	104	2	.290
1926	New York	A.L.	OF	152	495	139	184	11	.372
1927	New York	A.L.	OF	151	540	158	192	7	.356
1928	New York	A.L.	OF	154	536	163	173	4	.323
1929	New York	A.L.	OF	135	499	121	172	5	.345
1930	New York	A.L.	OF	145	518	150	186	10	.359
1931	New York	A.L.	OF	145	534	149	199	5	.373
1932	New York	A.L.	OF	132	457	120	156	2	.341
1933	New York	A.L.	OF	137	459	97	138	4	.301
1934	New York	A.L.	OF	125	365	78	105	1	.288
1935	Boston	N.L.	OF	28	72	13	13	0	.181
	Complete Major League Totals		22 Yrs.	2502	8399	2174	2873	123	.342

a Sold, July 8, to Boston. Reported sale price, $2,900.
b Optionally, to Providence, Aug. 15.
c Sold to New York. Reported sale price, $125,000.

	World Series Record		Pos.	G.	A.B.	R.	H.	S.B.	Avg.
1915	Boston	A.L.	PH	1	1	0	0	0	.000
1916	Boston	A.L.	P	1	5	0	0	0	.000
1918	Boston	A.L.	P	3	5	0	1	0	.200
1921	New York	A.L.	OF	6	16	3	5	2	.313
1922	New York	A.L.	OF	5	17	1	2	0	.118
1923	New York	A.L.	OF	6	19	8	7	0	.368
1926	New York	A.L.	OF	7	20	6	6	1	.300
1927	New York	A.L.	OF	4	15	4	6	1	.400
1928	New York	A.L.	OF	4	16	9	10	0	.625
1932	New York	A.L.	OF	4	15	6	5	0	.333
	World's Series Totals			41	129	37	42	4	.326

RUTH'S PITCHING RECORD

Year	Club	League	G.	IP.	W.	L.	Pct.	H.	R.	ER.	BB.	SO.	ERA.
1914	Balt.-Providence	I.L.	35	245	22	9	.709	210	88	......	101	139	......
1914	Boston	A.L.	4	22	2	1	.667	21	12	10	7	2	3.91
1915	Boston	A.L.	32	218	18	6	.750	166	80	59	85	112	2.44
1916	Boston	A.L.	44	324	23	12	.657	230	83	63	118	170	1.75
1917	Boston	A.L.	41	326	23	13	.639	244	93	73	108	128	2.02
1918	Boston	A.L.	20	166	13	7	.650	125	51	41	49	40	2.22
1919	Boston	A.L.	17	133	8	5	.615	148	59	44	58	30	2.97
1920	N. Y.	A.L.	1	4	1	0	1.000	3	4	2	2	0	4.50
1921	N. Y.	A.L.	2	9	2	0	1.000	14	10	4	10	2	4.00
1930	N. Y.	A.L.	1	9	1	0	1.000	11	3	3	3	2	3.00
1933	N. Y.	A.L.	1	9	1	0	1.000	12	5	5	3	0	5.00
	Major League Totals		163	1220	92	44	.667	974	400	304	443	486	2.24

The outstanding feature of Babe Ruth's matchless career was his home run record, 714 clouts, an unbelievable total. Here are a few brief highlights on where and when these homers were made.

Cities		Opposing Clubs Am. League		By Months		Pitchers	
New York	346	Detroit	123	April	48	Right Handers	493
Philadelphia	68	Philadelphia	108	May	133	Left Handers	221
Detroit	59	Chicago	98	June	140		
Boston	57	St. Louis	97	July	148		
St. Louis	55	Cleveland	92	August	124		
Cleveland	46	Boston	90	September	115		
Chicago	46	Washington	88	October	6		
Washington	34	New York	12				
Pittsburgh	3	Nat. League					
		Pittsburgh	3				
		New York	1				
		Brooklyn	1				
		Chicago	1				
	714		714		714		714

RUTH'S WORLD SERIES HOMERS

Date	Pitcher and Club	Men on Bases	Where
Oct. 9, 1921,	off Douglas (R), Giants	0	New York
Oct. 11, 1923,	off McQuillan (R), Giants	0	New York
Oct. 11, 1923,	off Bentley (L), Giants	0	New York
Oct. 15, 1923,	off Nehf (L), Giants	0	New York
Oct. 6, 1926,	off Rhem (R), Cardinals	0	St. Louis
Oct. 6, 1926,	off Rhem (R), Cardinals	0	St. Louis
Oct. 6, 1926,	off Bell (R), Cardinals	1	St. Louis
Oct. 10, 1926,	off Haines (R), Cardinals	0	New York
Oct. 7, 1927,	off Cvengros (L), Pirates	2	New York
Oct. 8, 1927,	off Hill (R), Pirates	1	New York
Oct. 9, 1928,	off Sherdel (L), Cardinals	0	St. Louis
Oct. 9, 1928,	off Sherdel (L), Cardinals	0	St. Louis
Oct. 9, 1928,	off Alexander (R), Cardinals	0	St. Louis
Oct. 1, 1932,	off Root (R), Cubs	2	Chicago
Oct. 1, 1932,	off Root (R), Cubs	0	Chicago

RUTH'S HOMERS WITH BASES FULL

Date	Pitcher and Club	Where
May 20, 1919,	off Davenport (R), Browns	St. Louis
June 30, 1919,	off Shawkey (R), Yankees	New York
July 18, 1919,	off Coumbe (L), Indians	Cleveland
Aug. 23, 1919,	off Dauss (R), Tigers	Detroit
July 6, 1922,	off Mails (L), Indians	New York
Sept. 24, 1925,	off Connally (R), White Sox	New York
Sept. 25, 1926,	off Vangilder (R), Browns	St. Louis
Sept. 27, 1927,	off Grove (L), Athletics	New York
Sept. 29, 1927,	off Hopkins (R), Senators	New York
July 3, 1929,	off Ruffing (R), Red Sox	New York
Aug. 6, 1929,	off Burke (L), Senators	New York
Aug. 7, 1929,	off Ehmke (R), Athletics	Philadelphia
Sept. 27, 1930,	off Earnshaw (R), Athletics	Philadelphia
Aug. 20, 1931,	off Hebert (L), Browns	St. Louis
May 21, 1932,	off Brown (L), Senators	New York
June 24, 1934,	off Jones (R), White Sox	New York

Courtesy The Baseball Magazine, N. Y. C.

Contents

Babe Ruth

1

The Drum Beater

Joe Engel had passed his fortieth birthday before he put his first elephant into a baseball park, but he had been a problem child long before that. Shortly after the turn of the century, when young Engel, as the son of a moderately prosperous saloon keeper in the nation's capital, reached the age of reason, it was evident that reasoning with young Joseph was going to be a man-sized job. There were, in the early 1900's in Washington, no such things as what have since become known as progressive schools. In the absence of these advanced educational and cultural adjuncts, Engel's parents developed a perfectly understandable concern over what was to become of their Joe.

Having no access to child psychologists, the Engels decided that they had a brat on their hands. They didn't, however, just reach the decision and let it go at that. Even in those days it was becoming fashionable for the boys and girls of the middle class to learn how to read and write. It wasn't that Joe was backward, either then or later. He possessed his full quota of intelligence, plus an amazing ingenuity. He had the capability to absorb education, but none of his instructors showed sufficient durability to absorb Joe. When it came to a question of taking young Joe or leaving him, they left him.

It so happened that a neighbor of the Engels, over a pot of tea and a platter of cookies, told Mrs. Engel about Mount St. Mary's, a prep school and college for boys and young men, situated high atop a rugged tor at Emmitsburg, Maryland. Emmitsburg was just south of the Pennsylvania state line, eleven miles from the historic battlefield at Gettysburg. The curriculum was presided over by secular priests and lay brothers and some of the more apt pupils went on to become seminarians and later men of God.

Although the Engels were not Catholics, Joe's mother had a high esteem for the educational gifts of the good fathers, particularly such representatives as were stationed at Mount St. Mary's. It had been truly said of them that they spared few rods and spoiled practically no children. Arrangements were made to enter Joe at Mount St. Mary's.

There are many who claim Joe presented the acid test to the teaching talents of the priests, others, including Joe himself, who insist that his years at Emmitsburg saved him from a life of crime. There was no doubt about the verdict when Engel descended from The Mount. He said "Ma'am" to his mother and "Sir" to his father and practically never wore his hat indoors.

While the priests at Mount St. Mary's succeeded in making a gentleman out of Joe, or a reasonable facsimile thereof, they planted in him no great love for the arts and sciences. He showed no particular desire to study Blackstone nor to spend Washington's hot and humid summers in an anatomical lab that he might one day swear to the oath of Hippocrates. His election of professions, although somewhat startling, was rather pleasing to his dad. Joe decided to become a baseball pitcher, although not a very good one, with the Washington club of the American League.

Nevertheless, Joe was happy and his dad was happy. Indeed, it became quite the dodge for the clients of his father's taproom, watching the ticker tape carrying the baseball results, to inform Engel, senior, that Joe was pitching that particular afternoon for Washington. Actually the pitcher would be Walter Johnson, but Joe's dad was never informed of the switch. As the great Sir Walter mowed down the opposition, and scoreless round after scoreless round was marked upon the blackboard in the saloon, the elder Engel, marveling at the talent that was his son's, would set up round after round on the bar for his cronies, also scoreless.

Apparently Joe's formative years under the good fathers at The Mount left no scars upon his soul, for he maintained a desultory correspondence with them through the years and was invited back to Emmitsburg one day to pitch for the alumni in a Commencement Day game. Joe was understandably proud of this request, since it was the only time on record that Joe was ever invited to pitch anywhere.

When Joe reached the playing field, there was a preliminary game in progress. The freshman squad of Mount St. Mary's was playing an orphanage from Baltimore, a team which bore the full title of St. Mary's Industrial Home for Boys. Pitching for the visitors was a tall and gangling kid, a left-hander with what Engel claimed was the most mature haircomb he ever saw on a kid. His hair, jet black, was clipped close on the sides, and "roached" on top, after a style affected by bartenders of the 90's.

"He really could wheel that ball in there," recalled Engel in later years. "And remember, I had been looking at Walter Johnson, who also was pretty quick. This boy with the trick haircut was just a great natural pitcher. He had everything and he must have struck out eighteen or twenty of the freshmen during the game."

When it came Joe's turn to pitch for the alumni against the varsity, he spotted the youngster from the orphanage seated in the stands. It would have been difficult not to have spotted him, for the big kid towered over most of the spectators and still wore his pitching costume. If that alone weren't sufficient to make him conspicuous, he carried a big bass drum and incessantly banged away on it, employing his left hand exclusively.

When the last batter had been retired, the last diploma awarded and the last platitudinal speech had died on the air, Engel grabbed a train back to Washington. It so happened that the same train was carrying the Oriole team of the International League back to Baltimore. Joe, as befitted his social status as a major leaguer, dropped into a seat in the day coach alongside of Jack Dunn, the Baltimore manager.

"Where you been working, Slick?" asked Dunn, as he watched Engel stuff his uniform roll into the baggage rack.

"Aw, just pitching against some college kids," replied Engel with what he assumed was becoming modesty.

"That's where you belong," said Dunn, who had no great regard for Joe's pitching skill and never took pains to conceal this lack of regard. "See anybody that looked any good?"

"Yeah," responded Joe, delighted to change the subject. "There was some orphan asylum from Baltimore playing in the first game and they had a young left-handed kid pitching for them who's got real stuff. He also can beat the hell out of a bass drum."

"You don't happen to remember his name, do you?" asked Dunn, reaching inside his coat for a pencil and old envelope.

"I think they called him Ruth," said Engel.

So far as is known, that night on the train, rattling from Emmitsburg to Baltimore and Washington, was the first time the name of Ruth was mentioned by anybody in professional baseball. It was ironical that Engel, who was later to become a professional scout for Washington and to uncover many a first-rate star for Clark Griffith, should have tipped off Dunn to the greatest ball player he was ever to see—free, gratis, and for nothing.

Ruth, of course, did not go to the Orioles and become a star instanter and forthwith. For one thing, Jack Dunn had more things on his mind than to go scouring the orphan asylums of Baltimore for a left-handed pitcher who also applied himself with gusto to a bass drum. Yet the paths of Dunn and Ruth were inextricably interwoven from that night on, even though neither knew it.

Among the many brothers who guided the destinies of the waifs at St. Mary's Industrial Home was a Brother Gilbert. He had been watching Ruth for nearly a decade and saw that the boy was an absolute fanatic about baseball. The lessons and the textbooks, the hours spent learning the rudiments of a trade meant little to Big George. He had the intelligence to assimilate them but not the desire. Except when he was playing baseball, or beating the biggest and noisiest drum he could find, Big George was bored. He bored easily in those days as, indeed, he did in later years.

Baseball was all that could hold Ruth's attention and Brother Gilbert recognized not only this but that Big George was an exceptionally gifted and able performer. Before any of the other brothers at the institution with the exception of Brother Matthias, the coach, even before Ruth himself, Brother Gilbert realized that the boy had the skill to become a professional ball player.

Ruth, when he first played ball on any of the several teams at

St. Mary's, had been that *rara avis,* a left-handed catcher. Catching was, and is, rugged work on kid teams, with protective equipment at an absolute minimum, and it took a sturdy boy to be a catcher. Big George was all of that. As he grew older, about fifteen or sixteen, he found his *métier* in pitching. None of the teams facing Big George, either from within the school or from the outside, could stand up against his pitching. He rarely fanned less than a dozen a game and the average number of strikeouts ran closer to twenty.

It was about this time that Brother Gilbert decided to write a letter to Jack Dunn, asking that Ruth be given a trial with the Orioles. It took more than one letter, but Dunn finally came out to St. Mary's. He saw Big George and liked what he saw. To those of us who knew Ruth only when he was established as a major league home run hitter, it is hard to picture the boy Dunn saw that day at "The Home," as St. Mary's was euphemistically known to Baltimoreans.

To begin with, Ruth was a kid. That in itself is hard to visualize. He was about seventeen, tall and gangly, painfully thin almost everywhere except across his chest and shoulders, which even then were showing signs of massiveness. Everybody has read, and more than once, that Ruth was never anything but an overgrown kid, even in the days when he was spraying home runs all over the American landscape, but in appearance Ruth was a man, a powerful, peculiarly shaped man.

Dunn had heard about Big George before. He heard about him by letter from Brother Gilbert, by word of mouth from Baltimore citizens who had seen or heard about his pitching, and he had heard about him from Joe Engel that summer night in 1913, pounding along in the day coach between Emmitsburg and Baltimore.

Dunn couldn't miss hearing about Ruth, any more than he could miss hearing about any other promising youth within walking distance of Baltimore. For Dunn, at that time, had succeeded to the mantle worn so flamboyantly by John Joseph McGraw a decade or so before. When McGraw moved his talents, and most of his Orioles, to wider and lusher pastures, Dunn, or Dunnie as everybody called him, assumed McGraw's position with Baltimore baseball fans. Indeed, as time went on, legends sprang up about Dunnie which made him a sort of lower-case McGraw.

Ruth pitched for Dunn's edification. Big George was not dressed in baseball flannels but wore a pair of blue denim overalls, which was standard dress for all the orphans at St. Mary's, save on Sundays when they attended Mass in the chapel on the grounds. Ruth was growing out of the overalls, as he was growing out of everything at St. Mary's, and the original dark blue of the denims had faded to a sort of wistful pastel. Dunnie, neither then nor ever, had an eye for sartorial grandeur. He saw Ruth pitch and he was satisfied, even to the point of making a mental note that Engel wasn't as much of a harum-scarum as he had thought.

After the game, Dunnie and Brother Gilbert sat quietly in the latter's office, lounging self-consciously in the battered and time-scarred chairs, each waiting for the other to speak. It was Brother Gilbert who, Eliza-like, negotiated the first conversational ice-floe.

"What do you think, John?" he ventured.

Apparently John thought a great deal, for he didn't reply immediately. Dunnie was not accustomed to dealing for his baseball chattels with men of the cloth. He would have known how to act with another baseball man, to knock the product and express a total lack of interest and then, at the very last minute, to offer to take the ball player off the latter's hands out of sheer sympathy and only because the milk of human kindness welled deep in his breast, quite deep.

Dunnie drew a deep breath and took the plunge.

"What do you want for him, Brother?" asked the leader of the Orioles.

"What do I want for him?" repeated the good Xaverian brother, puzzled. "Sure, John, he isn't mine to sell. All I want for him is a good home, proper care and the chance for him to make somebody of himself in the world, no more and no less."

Dunnie and the brother talked at great length after that modest speech. Jack arranged to sign formal papers, acting as Ruth's guardian, and to pay the boy a salary of $600 for the season of 1914. Big George was to be Dunnie's ward and responsibility first, and a southpaw for the Orioles afterward.

Ruth apparently took Dunn's guardianship literally, for when the Orioles assembled for training at Fayetteville, N. C., the following spring, he trotted puppy-like on to the practice field at Jack's heels. Big George, indeed, resembled a puppy in more ways than one—he

Keystone

The Orioles come home to roost. Ruth with his first manager, Jack Dunn (center), and Jack Bentley, at a charity game in the Polo Grounds for which Babe had been loaned to the Giants to play against Baltimore. Bentley, like Ruth, had been a southpaw pitcher for Dunn.

was growing, he was awkward and, above all, he was anxious to please.

It was on this first day of practice that Ruth was to draw the nickname which was to stick to him for all the days and years of his life, the most famous nickname in the history of American sports and one which was to make his baptismal name of George all but forgotten. Almost from that day on, nobody else ever addressed Ruth as anything but "Babe," his wife, his teammates, his managers, the sports writers, the fans and the non-fans and even presidents of the United States.

Baseball has no special niche in its Hall of Fame for the man who first tagged Ruth as "Babe" and you can pore over records for hours without discovering his first name, or even the position he held with the Orioles. His name was Stienman and he was a coach for Dunnie.

For posterity let it be recorded that when Ruth arrived on the practice field at Fayetteville that March day in 1914, trotting along after Dunnie, it was Stienman who observed, "Here comes Jack with his newest babe."

It has been Babe Ruth ever since. He had to become seriously ill in January of 1947 before even so staid a journal as the New York *Times* could recall that his full name was George Herman Erhardt Ruth.

About the Erhardt in Ruth's name there always has been considerable mystery and Babe himself has never been able to do anything to clear it up. The only thing about it of which Ruth is definite is the spelling. When Brooklyn came up with a sensational young pitcher named Rube Ehrhardt in the season of 1924, someone commented on the similarity of the names.

"Mine has only one 'h,' " explained Babe in what was probably the first, last and only time he ever set himself up as an authority on orthography.

Most of those who knew Ruth when he first came into the major leagues took it for granted that Erhardt had been his family name before he was picked off the streets of Baltimore and sent to St. Mary's Industrial Home. Some say that his parents were named Gearhardt, but Babe persistently stuck to Erhardt.

Ruth never talked of his early life. Although he always maintained his friendship with Brother Matthias, life for Ruth began the day he joined the Orioles. He never looked back any further than that. In what purported to be an autobiography, published in the early 1920's, Ruth once referred to a childhood on the waterfront streets of Baltimore, a rough, tough childhood of the type that Hollywood, with its usual brashness, attempted to make appetizing in a series of celluloid monstrosities featuring the Dead End Kids.

It wasn't a nice life and there are reasons for believing the Babe couldn't remember much of it, even if he wished, for he was at "The Home" when he was seven. Legend has it that Babe's mother, supposedly named Ruth, died either in childbirth or while he was still an infant and that his father was killed some few years later. On the other hand, there were some of the Babe's Red Sox teammates who remember Ruth's father, or at least a man who said he was Ruth's father, showing up at the ball park in Washington one day when Ruth was playing there.

Perhaps the best example of the misty veil hanging over the Babe's childhood came when he applied for a passport to make a baseball barnstorming tour of the Orient. All the record books listed his natal day as February 7, 1894, yet when a birth certificate for Ruth was unearthed in Baltimore as a passport credential, the date of his birth was given as February 6, 1895, a discrepancy of 364 days.

Ruth continued to celebrate his birthday on February 7, and never worried much whether he was 45 or 46, 52 or 53.

"What difference does it make now?" he would ask.

There is every bit as much chance of Ruth being correct as there is of the birth certificate issued by Baltimore's municipal authorities. In the 1890's, vital statistics weren't checked and cross-checked in the manner which was to become fashionable later. And, remember, that Ruth didn't come bawling into this world in the antiseptic, tile-walled delivery room of a maternity hospital, with a white-aproned obstetrician and several aides and anesthetists standing by. He was born in a house in Baltimore and the delivery was no doubt performed by a general practitioner, whose unpaid bills outnumbered his prescriptions, or a young ambulance intern summoned by a passing policeman. In any case, there would be no rush to record the event for posterity. It was just another birth in a section of the city which already had far more than its quota. Great men had been born in humbler surroundings before.

From the very first time Ruth had two silver dollars of his own to rub against each other in his pocket, it was evident that he was destined for unusual things. It was evident, also, that Dunn's ward wasn't to tag at his heels very long. Out of his first earnings as a Baltimore pitcher, Babe bought himself a motorcycle of fire-wagon red, which he used to drive around the streets of that city at a furious pace, stepping up the tempo of Baltimore's traffic considerably.

Dunn didn't have to worry about Ruth and the red motorcycle very long. Babe had a natural flair for pitching baseballs. He showed all the earmarks of a great star almost from the very first time he donned an Oriole uniform. One of his most remarkable baseball achievements, and one which has been entirely overlooked, is that Ruth, still in his 'teens, was able to come out of an orphanage and, with no previous professional experience or coaching, become a winning pitcher in the International League, then, as now, only a cut below the majors in playing skill.

Ruth became a star as soon as he was able to play professionally. In April, he made his first start as an Oriole and shut out Buffalo, 6 to 0. Playing second for the Bisons that day was Joe McCarthy, who went 0-for-4 against the young left-hander. Catching for Buffalo was Paul Krichell, Yankee scout, who made one single in four tries against Babe. Ruth himself hit two singles, one on his very first time at bat in organized ball.

The Federal League had muscled in on Dunnie's Baltimore territory and, although his Orioles were making a runaway of the International League race, the fans preferred to see the Feds play. When it reached the point where there were less than twenty people in the park Jack decided to sell his ball players. He sold Ruth, Ernie Shore and Ben Egan to the Red Sox in July. Joe Lannin, Red Sox owner, is reported to have paid $8500 for the trio. Babe's price was listed as $2900.

Boston bought Ruth strictly as a pitcher, for he hit no home runs as an Oriole. The Sox looked Babe over, pitched him, and then shipped him to Providence to help Bill Donovan's club overhaul Baltimore and win the International League pennant.

With the pennant won by Providence, Boston recalled Ruth to finish out the American League season. He never played another minor league game and remained in the majors, as an active player, for twenty-two seasons. The big fellow won two games for the Red Sox in 1914, while his combined pitching record with Baltimore and Providence in the International League was twenty-two victories and nine defeats. Thus, six months out of "The Home," Dunnie's Babe was winning on the big wheel. Ruth, incidentally, never had a losing season as a pitcher, even nineteen years later when the Yankees pitched him in one of the closing days of the 1933 season, merely as a box-office attraction. He pitched nine innings and won, beating the Red Sox.

Don't get the idea the Red Sox welcomed Big George when he came back from Providence. Ball players were rugged individualists back

Acme

The Kid's last stand. In his final start as a pitcher, Ruth pitched the Yankees to a 6 to 5 victory over the Red Sox at the Stadium, October 1, 1933. The Babe never had a losing season as a pitcher.

in 1914, and for a good many years later. A rookie coming to the majors was given the same cool reception which would be extended to a probationer from a leper colony. Babe, even then, fancied himself as a hitter, although he had batted less than .250 in the International League. He tried to take his turn in batting practice, or perhaps more than his turn. When he came to his locker in the Red Sox clubhouse the next morning, he found his bats neatly sawed into sections. Youngsters weren't supposed to muscle in on the closed shop maintained by the veterans.

Until his later years, when he grew broodingly bitter over the inescapable fact that professional baseball had closed and bolted the doors on him, Ruth had the happy faculty of wearing the world as a loose garment. His unhappy childhood, his years at "The Home" all faded behind him. The closed circle the Red Sox presented to Babe didn't worry him an iota. They could have sawed up all the bats that ever came out of Louisville but they weren't freezing out the Babe.

Within a year, Ruth was one of the Red Sox gang. At nineteen he had a car and a wife, a sixteen-year-old waitress named Helen Woodford. They went on the bowling parties with the other Red Sox players and their wives, notably Jack Barry and Mrs. Barry, a school teacher. Completely uninhibited, the Babe was as much at home with the Red Sox as if he had spent his entire life with them.

When Ruth was purchased by Joe Lannin for Boston, Bill Carrigan, Old Rough, wasted no time in getting a look at the young left-hander. Tradition has it that Babe, after a sleepless night on the train from Baltimore to Boston, was started in a game against Cleveland the day he arrived. He won his first American League game by a score of 4 to 3, proof positive that Lannin had bought no lemon and that Joe Engel and the Xaverian Brothers had been right in their early appraisal of the boy.

Keystone

Babe and his first wife, the former Helen Woodring, whom he married shortly after he became a regular with the Red Sox.

It would be romantic to speculate that Ruth's sleepless night en route to Boston was caused by his concern over his future. The proper touch would be to have the young orphan reading into the rhythmic click of the wheels some fanciful refrain, such as Dick Whittington imagined he heard in the chimes of Big Ben as he was about to leave London in despair. Such speculation, however, is out of order with anyone who knows Ruth. If Big George spent a sleepless night, it was because he was sitting up in a day coach. The Babe never looked into the future, any more than he looked back at the past. He had in himself that complete confidence to be found only in men of destiny and extroverts. Babe was both.

One point which should be made clear in any story of Ruth is that he was a completely natural ball player from the time he first put on a left-handed catcher's mitt at St. Mary's Industrial Home. He was taught little because he didn't have to be taught much. The Babe pitched and won the first big league game he ever saw, a distinction few major leaguers can claim.

Ruth was an instinctive ball player. He required no more tutoring in the game than a seal pup would in swimming. Where some ball players, like Ty Cobb for instance, owe their success to great powers of observation and to study, Babe came full-blown. When he was pitching he neither knew nor cared whether the batter who faced him stood at the right or left side of the plate, and when he was hitting he never took the time to distinguish between southpaws and right-handers. They all looked alike to the Babe.

Having seen Ruth pitch that day at Emmitsburg, Engel went on his merry way. When his pitching no longer filled the stern heart of Clark Griffith with admiration, Joe became a scout for the ball club and finally wound up operating the Chattanooga farm club for Washington in the Southern Association. It was here Engel finally found an outlet for his manifold talents. He operated not only the ball club but a radio station and a night club on the side.

Showmanship is a much-abused term in sports. Sometimes it consists of nothing more than a raw affront to the sensibilities of the public. Often it is a shrewd attempt to bring spectators to see something they have no desire to see. It is as difficult to find a happy medium for showmanship in sports as it is to find the proper niche for the radio commercial. Whatever the place of showmanship in the history of sports, it was Joe Engel who first brought it into baseball. Through his diabolical machinations, he eventually brought all of Chattanooga's baseball public, a segment of that city's population which never was quite large enough to satisfy Joe, to a complete state of flux. They never were quite sure what they were going to see when they went to the Lookouts' ball park. Just as Joe was the first professional baseball player ever to see Ruth in a ball game, so was he the first to bring the sawdust and the tanbark to baseball. In a way, Engel might be called the poor man's Larry MacPhail.

Engel staged elephant hunts in the ball park at Chattanooga. He once traded an infielder for a Tom turkey. He gave away automobiles and hired swing bands to bemuse the bewildered Chattanooga fans, or perhaps to take their mind off his ball club. He brought bank night and the country store to baseball. When the customers stayed away in droves, he caused a huge sign to be posted over the entrance which read: "This Park is Not Quarantined Because of Polio."

Nevertheless, the greatest lure Engel ever put before the baseball-minded citizens of Chattanooga was Babe Ruth, who played there many times in exhibition games with the Yankees. Babe outdrew the elephants and the chinaware, the jazz bands and silk stockings, for Babe was baseball, pure and unadulterated.

Engel likes to recall a second conversation he had with Jack Dunn, just about a year after the one they had in the day-coach rattling from Emmitsburg to Baltimore. It was now early 1914 and Ruth was an Oriole.

"I see," said Engel to Dunnie with the smug air of one who is sure of his ground, "that you signed that big fellow I told you about."

"Who?" asked Dunn, who selected his ball players with far more care than he did his pronouns.

"Don't give me that," said Engel heatedly. "The left-handed kid that I told you I saw up at The Mount. The kid who pitched and beat the hell out of the bass drum afterward."

"Oh, him," answered Dunn lightly. "Yeah, I signed him. And let me tell you, Joe, he's a very mediocre drummer."

2

The Tinsel Crown

Through the years, man and boy, beard and goatee, George Bernard Shaw found more gold in snobbishness than Ward MacAllister ever dreamed could be mined in that particular field. It was the happy habit of GBS to pretend that no subject or individual with which he wasn't wholly familiar could possibly be of interest to anybody. By expressing a sneering pity for the entire human race, Shaw attracted sufficient attention to his undeniable talents to store away great shovelfuls of the wealth he found so contemptible.

One thing Shaw learned early in his career was that he could rib his American cousins more profitably than he could his neighbors and relatives in the British Isles. Americans rose to the bait like undernourished trout; there were more of them and they had more money. GBS rarely fired a blank round in the direction of these United States.

Back in the middle 1920's, when Calvin Coolidge was confusing muteness with statesmanship, and getting away with it too, Shaw felt impelled to make a remark about Babe Ruth. Ruth was an international figure then, in a sport which wasn't played anywhere but in the Americas, and an itinerant American journalist asked the patron saint of the vegetarians what he thought of Babe Ruth, who was getting fabulous sums for knocking a baseball farther than anyone ever had before.

Keystone

Maybe George Bernard Shaw didn't know the Bambino but this gendarme in Gay Paree did. With Ruth are Mrs. Ruth and daughter, Julia, on their way home after a world tour in 1934.

Although their talents lay in somewhat dissimilar fields, Shaw had heard of Ruth, but it is extremely dubious if Ruth had ever heard of Shaw. GBS recognized the question as a God-sent opportunity to send another Shavian barb flying in the direction of America and to be rewarded with columns of free publicity, so he turned the question on the questioner and spoke thusly:

"Who is this Baby Ruth?" he asked. "And what does she do?"

Shaw hit the bull's-eye. Hundreds of thousands of Americans paused in outraged indignation, amazed that there was anybody anywhere in the English-speaking world who not only didn't know Ruth, but didn't know what he did, or that his nickname was Babe, not Baby. That Shaw should pretend ignorance of Ruth's sex and his profession seemed nothing more or less than a calculated insult. It was, of course, and Shaw undoubtedly permitted himself a polite titter behind his beard when he saw how big America was taking it.

It reflects no great credit on America's lust for culture to state that then, as now, there were more Americans who knew of Babe Ruth than of George Bernard Shaw. A photograph of Ruth, placed in any shopkeeper's window from Fifth Avenue to Main Street, would be recognized by more people than one of Shaw, and it must be admitted that if Ruth and Shaw have anything in common at all it is that both are blessed with unusual physiognomies. You would never mistake either for your Uncle Harry.

Baseball has had outstanding personalities since Ruth—its Joe DiMaggios, its Ted Williamses, Rogers Hornsbys, Hack Wilsons and Bobby Fellers. Crowds have clamored around admission booths at ball parks to see these performers in numbers almost as large as those which stormed the portals to see the Babe. Yet of none of them can it be said, as it can be said of the Babe, that he broke up as many games with a pencil as he did with a bat.

There was a time when the Yankees and Ruth made exhibition baseball an integral part of baseball receipts. Barnstorming on the way home from Florida, the Yankees played all through Texas and Oklahoma, the Carolinas, Georgia, Virginia and Louisiana. During the regular season, the club might have an open date on its schedule, but it never was open in the literal sense of the term for the Yankees always were playing somebody, someplace, were it Binghamton or Montreal, Toronto or Danbury or any of the various Springfields, Massachusetts or Missouri, Illinois or Ohio.

Gradually these games came to take on a phenomenal sameness—none of them were ever finished. The crowds were always so extensive that segments of the cash customers had to deploy themselves around the playing field, there never being sufficient room in the stands to accommodate all of those who wished to see the mighty Ruth.

Ropes or, in their absence, a recruited militia of ball park employees would mark the outfield boundaries and restrain the curious. Since the opposition was invariably the local team, able neither in skill nor experience to cope with the Yankees, the score was invariably lopsided in favor of the major leaguers.

In the latter innings, somewhere around the seventh, a youngster

Keystone

Ruth entertained 7500 boys in an exhibition game at Los Angeles and was gleefully mobbed at the finale.

inevitably would slip his leash, get under the ropes and, eluding the impromptu constabulary, dash out to where Ruth was playing, holding forth an object to be autographed, a baseball, a program or maybe only a scrap of paper. The Babe would obligingly shed his familiar white fielder's mitt (he wrote right-handed) and, using his knee as a prop, scrawl his signature on the proffered object.

Hardly would this task be completed before another youngster emboldened by the successful daring of the first, would be at the Babe's side, importuning his signature once more. Again Ruth would oblige, but this time there would be no opportunity to return his glove to his right hand for there would be others around Babe. Adults would have joined the horde of autograph-seekers by now. The throng would increase rapidly as whole sections of the overflow crowd clustered around Ruth.

In less time than it takes to describe only the top of Ruth's cap could be espied from the stands, as he was completely engulfed in a sea of admirers. Sometimes the fans who were unable to get out of the stands would pelt the crowd on the field with cushions and wadded up programs and sometimes not, but the result was always the same. The game was over. It was never possible to clear the field and resume hostilities once Ruth's devotees had taken possession of him.

So regularly was this scene repeated at Yankee exhibition games that some of the more cynical minded claimed the enthusiasm was synthetically inspired. Charley O'Leary, one of Miller Huggins' first aides with the Yankees, was singled out as the agent provocateur who would urge the first autograph-seeker to venture to Ruth's side, after which nature would inevitably take its course.

There is evidence enough to support the fact that during at least one exhibition game O'Leary encouraged a juvenile spectator to seek Ruth's signature, which was the equivalent of having the little Dutch boy remove his thumb from the dike. This was understandable enough. The many exhibitions were merely an added chore to the Yankees and the sooner the performance was ended, the sooner the players would be at the dining table. On the other hand, I covered at least a dozen such exhibitions at which the demonstration was spontaneous and not inspired from within. People just liked to get close to the big fellow.

When Ruth entered a Manhattan hospital in November of 1946, there was a routine announcement that he had gone there for a check-up and for treatment of a sinus condition. When it became apparent that this was more than a routine visit and that Babe would not be home for Christmas, the hospital was deluged with telephone calls and Ruth began to receive baskets of letters daily. The longer he stayed in the hospital, the more phone calls poured in and the more numerous his mail became.

By the time Ruth left the hospital, in mid-February, crowds lined the streets hours before he was scheduled to make his departure. New York City's finest had to throw a cordon of blue about the hospital entrance to enable him to reach the automobile which was to carry him to his apartment. It was a scene totally unlike any ever before inspired by a sports personage. It was testimony that the big fellow, who had played his last major league game nearly a dozen years before, still retained his unprecedented grip on the baseball world.

Ruth's illness in the winter of 1946-47 wasn't the type calculated to arouse public excitement. He entered the hospital quietly enough and neither press associations nor sports editors set up the macabre machinery of the newspaper death watch, which is usually instituted when a celebrity takes to his bed. Interest in Babe's condition grew gradually but the cumulative effect resulted in a daily bulletin in every paper in the land.

In many ways the intense interest in Ruth's welfare was a greater tribute to his peculiar niche in the American sports world than anything which had gone before, even when he was making and breaking home run records. For now Ruth was a man in his early fifties, long since passed from the competitive scene. His last major league games had been those ill-advised few he played with the Boston Braves some twelve years before; his last association with a professional ball club had been the few months he served with Brooklyn as a coach back in 1938. And it was 1947 when crowds thronged the streets around the hospital to catch a glimpse of him on his way home.

Not the least amazing feature of the thousands of cheering letters the Babe received during his illness and convalescence was that the majority of them were from youngsters, scarcely any of whom could have remembered him as a player and none of whom could have named any of his contemporaries in his hey-day with the mighty Yankees. They hadn't been born when Ruth had smashed his record-breaking tôtal of sixty homers in 1927. Few celebrities, ball players or crooners, actors or politicians, achieve a grip on the public which extends beyond their active and productive years.

Ruth was one ball player who could steal the spotlight without his monkey suit. During the 1933 World Series between Washington and the Giants, the Babe went along as a non-combatant. He was ostensibly covering the games for the Christy Walsh Syndicate, but his duties were merely to sit in the press box and communicate his observations to Bill Slocum or Ford Frick, who then whipped them into readable shape for Babe's public. He touched neither typewriter nor pencil.

Before one of the games in Washington, Kirk Miller, a Washington sports editor, arranged for the visiting writers to have an audience with Franklin Delano Roosevelt, then in the first year of his first term in the White House. When we were assembled outside the Oval Room, the protocol of meeting the President was explained to us.

The procedure was for the writers to advance single-file to the entrance, where the President would meet us. We were to announce our names and our newspaper affiliations to Miller, who then would present us to the chief executive. Although many of us knew Kirk well, there was to be no variance of the routine—we were still to announce our names and our newspapers in a loud and clear voice. This was to protect from embarrassment any among us who were not on familiar terms with Miller.

There was a slight stir when Babe Ruth, in tow of Bill Slocum, his current ghost writer and longtime friend, joined our group. None of us, as far as I know, considered Ruth a working newspaperman. Although most of us, particularly those who had traveled with the Yanks, considered Babe one of the mob, there were some who resented his presence. Some newspapermen can be as touchy about the sanctity of their profession as the Grand Lama of Tibet.

The door to the Oval Room opened and a presidential secretary announced that FDR would now meet us. The President, affable and smiling, began talking of the third game of the Series, in which Earl Whitehill had shut out the Giants and at which he, the President, had been present. Suddenly, he spotted Ruth in the queue.

"Well, Babe," broke off the President, "how are you? This is a surprise!"

"I'm fine, thanks, Mr. President," mumbled the Babe.

"You know, boys," said Roosevelt, turning to the group at large and chuckling as one about to retell an anecdote he personally enjoys telling, "this is not the first time Babe and I have crossed paths.

"I remember back in 1920, when I was running for Vice-President on the ticket with James M. Cox. I was scheduled to make a speech in October in Binghamton, New York. Our chances were never deemed very good and when I reached the railroad station I was surprised to see a large, if not very enthusiastic crowd, not only in the station itself, but in the streets beyond. The police had difficulty in getting us through the crowd at the station and when we reached the hotel there was another crowd around the entrances and in the lobby itself, a crowd which rather reluctantly parted to allow us to reach the elevators.

"When I got to my room, I turned to one of my companions and said, 'What an amazing turn-out. We may not be as badly off as some people think.'

"One of the locals on the Democratic committee said, 'I don't like to discourage you or disappoint you, sir, but that crowd didn't turn out for your speech or for the Democratic Party. Babe Ruth and his barnstormers are expected in shortly to play a ball game here.' "

The Babe rumbled an apologetic laugh when Roosevelt finished speaking and gave a deprecatory shrug of his shoulders as if to say, "It happens all the time."

It isn't just an idle phrase to say that Ruth was internationally famous, for he was. Crowds followed him about the streets of Japan when he visited there with a barnstorming troupe of major leaguers. In the early fighting on Guadalcanal, when most of the Nips opposing the Marines were English-speaking, they sought to taunt our boys into exposing themselves by screeching derogatory remarks about Babe Ruth.

Keystone

When Babe arrived in Tokyo in 1934, with touring major leaguers, the Japanese greeted him hysterically.

Infantile as this procedure was, and happily ineffectual, it offers an inkling of the impression Ruth and his home runs had made on the Japanese mind. Thousands of Japanese had seen the Babe play ball, thousands more had read about him. Their assumption was that he must be enshrined as a national hero in the United States and that any insult to his name would make the Americans come out fighting, regardless of consequences.

One other war story indirectly concerning Ruth came from the beachhead at Anzio, in those dark and perilous days shortly after the initial landings had been made and the men on the beach were fighting to maintain their foothold. There were no lines, in the accepted sense of the term, and the challenge and password were changed daily as a precaution against Nazi infiltration. On one occasion, the challenge was "Yankees" and the password was "Ruth."

This wasn't intended as a tribute to the Babe at all, but was simply an effort to get a combination of words as typically American as possible ("Chesterfield" and "cigarette" were another combination) and a relationship between these words which would be alien to a German. The tribute to Babe, if any, was in linking his name with the Yankees, although it had been ten years since he had worn a Yankee uniform. To the GI's on the Italian beachhead, Ruth and the Yankees seemed as natural a combination as ham and eggs, although it is doubtful if many of the embattled soldiers ever had seen the Babe in a Yankee uniform.

Ruth's personal appearance was such that he could be readily recognized by anyone who had ever seen his photograph. The Babe was so huge he stood out in any group, even among his teammates and ball players, incidentally, run to bigger physiques than any other athletic group.

Nobody ever had to be told which player was Ruth, even people entering a ball park for the first time. His round head, his button nose, his huge jowls, which obscured his square jaw, made Babe's face one among a million. The broad shoulders and pipestem legs, the surprisingly thin arms and, in later years, the overhanging bay window, all were part of the Ruthian trademark.

Off the field, Ruth had one sartorial quirk—he never wore a hat. Those who knew Babe well and who traveled with him just can't imagine him wearing a fedora. A derby on Ruth would have been as amazing a sight as spats on a Yaqui Indian. For a time Ruth affected a stiff-brim sailor straw but an unfortunate (and unpretty) experience with his teammate, Mike McNally, caused Babe to discard one particular straw hat and there is no record that he ever bought another.

Brown Bros.

As if the Yankees did not schedule enough exhibition games, Ruth went barnstorming with Lou Gehrig after one season, piloting the Bustin' Babes against the Larrupin' Lous. It was Babe's only shot at managing.

Ruth's headgear, from the early 1920's on, was a cap. And on him it looked good. Babe's tan polo coat, with matching camel's hair cap, were standard equipment for the big fellow at all outdoor appearances in the fall and winter. He went hatless, or rather, capless, in the summer.

For a celebrity, Ruth appeared in more small towns than anybody else. More baseball fans, as distinguished from major league fans, saw the Babe than they did any other ball player. This, of course, was due to exhibition baseball, both the games sponsored by the Yankees and his own independent barnstorming tours. And these fans were rarely disappointed by the big fellow, who hit barnstorming homers all the way from Lewiston, Maine, to Seattle, Washington, from Tampa, Florida, to Tulsa, Oklahoma.

Ruth is the only ball player who couldn't eat in public without starting a riot. You could find any of the later stars, Bobby Feller or Ted Williams, Joe DiMaggio or Stan Musial, in the coffee shop or dining room at whatever hotel the club was stopping or in the dining car on the train. Babe didn't dare expose himself. He was forced to take his meals in the privacy of his room or in his compartment on the train.

This seclusion which was forced upon Ruth irked Joe McCarthy in the four seasons he managed the Yankees with Babe on the club. In those days, the Yankees traveled by train. When the airplane came in, McCarthy went out, although the two aren't necessarily cause and effect. Just what mysterious system of jungle telegraphy was employed always has remained a puzzle to those who traveled with the club, but whenever the train bearing the Yankees paused to water the engine, people materialized as though out of the ground. People, mind you, not just kids, but grown men and women, all stretching and craning their necks for a peep at the great man.

Not infrequently the curious boarded the train during its brief pause and dashed through the aisles crying, "Where is he? Where's the Babe?" They brushed by other Yankee players as though they didn't exist—Lou Gehrig, Bob Meusel, Tony Lazzeri and Herb Pennock. They also brushed by Joe McCarthy. And that was the rub. Miller Huggins never minded it and Bob Shawkey, in the one year the managerial toga slipped and slithered about his shoulders, didn't mind it either, because he had long been inured to it through his years as a teammate of the Babe.

McCarthy never did become used to the exclusiveness with which Ruth was paid homage at these hamlets. For all his years in baseball, for all his undeniable intelligence in the directing of a ball club and his deep understanding in handling men, Joe never got around to understanding that peculiar genus of *homo sapiens,* the American baseball fan.

It was, of course, merely a minor and passing irritant to McCarthy and is mentioned only because it serves again to emphasize the peculiar position Ruth gained in the public eye. The average fan considers it a rare privilege to see any of his heroes in the flesh and off the field. A man of standing and stature in his community will gawk popeyed at a utility infielder if he happens to be dining a few tables away in a public restaurant. That these fans at the wayside stops of the Yankees would dash blithely by other headline performers in their eagerness to see Ruth can be explained only by the fact that the presence of the big fellow blinded them to the presence of all others. Who would bother to look at a prince when the king was just around the corner?

That Ruth should go to Hollywood was inevitable, since Hollywood couldn't come to him. He made some motion pictures, going all the way back to the old silent days with Anna Q. Nilsson, and they were among the most incredible films to come from that incredible land. Like so many athletes before him who turned to acting, the Babe found himself in over his head. The only time Ruth ever distinguished himself in a motion picture was after he was all through as a ball player, when he played a bit part in *Pride of the Yankees,* the story of Lou Gehrig's life. Ruth played himself—the only role he ever was able to play.

Ruth ventured on to the airwaves on several occasions. Here again he was out of his element and for the very same reason. He wasn't allowed to play himself. Babe had trouble reading his lines, yet people listened to him because he was Babe Ruth. One of his early programs, sponsored by a cereal company, was so successful that he wasn't rehired at the end of his initial thirteen weeks.

This incongruity was caused by the fact that Ruth, despite his falter-

Press Association

A scene from Ruth's first movie in 1927. It had to do with love and baseball—naturally. Babe got the homer and the gal.

ing delivery, was such an excellent radio salesman that he sold himself right out of a job! Listeners were required to send in a certain number of box tops, together with a few coins, to receive autographed baseballs or other diamond paraphernalia. A survey conducted by Babe's sponsors, on the strength of the box top returns, convinced them that at the end of thirteen weeks every 'teen-aged kid within the sound of Ruth's voice had a sufficient quantity of that particular breakfast food

Culver Service

Kids throng NBC studio to watch the Babe broadcast for a cereal company in 1934. The youngsters so enthusiastically supported the product Ruth plugged that he was soon out of a job.

on hand to last him until he attained his majority. The saturation point having been attained, the program was dropped.

Ruth was an ardent, and avid, golfer and he once took part in one of the strangest golfing exhibitions in the long history of that royal and ancient game. Certainly there never was a golf match, before or since, which attracted such a strange gallery as that which gathered to see Babe perform one Sunday afternoon at the Fresh Meadow Golf Club in Queens, New York City.

Bill Corum, Hearst sports columnist, drummed up the match to raise money for a fund for the underprivileged. Babe Didrikson, Mrs. Sylva Annenberg and John Montague were the other contestants or, more accurately, performers, for at no time did this bizarre golf exhibition take on any aspect of a contest. It had been presumed that

Press Association

Just before the storm! The Bam and Mysterious Montague play a practice round at Fresh Meadow. A few days later at their charity match, Ruth was almost mobbed by admirers.

Montague, because of his unusual reputation, would be the magnet.

Montague came from Hollywood with countless Paul Bunyan legends whirling around him. He was, to hear some tell it, the greatest golfer in the world. He was also the strongest man in the world. For years, it seemed, he had desired, above all else, privacy. This was why the rest of the world had been kept so long in ignorance of his amazing skill. He could drive a ball 300 yards and plant a chip shot in a derby hat, blindfolded, at fifty paces. Only a privileged few had ever seen him perform. It developed, when Montague was eventually exposed to the public light, that he also was something of a mountebank.

This November Sunday in 1937 turned out to be a beautiful fall day. It also turned out practically all Broadway on the fairways of Fresh Meadow. People who had never seen a golf match before, or since, showed up, not because they had the faintest conception of the game or any appreciation for it but merely because it meant an opportunity to see Babe Ruth close up.

Mysterious Montague was practically ignored and La Didrikson was just a girl who had been a track star. Mrs. Annenberg was merely a lady with a golf stick. Ruth was the big show. When Babe stepped to the tee, his admirers stepped with him. They practically breathed on his neck when he addressed the ball. They lined up in front of the tee, leaving Ruth an alley of about twenty feet in which to place his drive. That Ruth might hook or slice his shot never occurred to them.

It was evident before the first ball was hit that this was a match which would never be finished. This particular gallery had never heard of golf marshals or their functions. They just stood anywhere which afforded them the best view of Ruth, even though it happened to be directly in front of him as he was about to play a shot. It wasn't an unruly crowd, just a happily ignorant one.

After struggling through nine holes during which dozens of spectators had miraculously escaped decapitation, the match was called off and the gallery trudged happily back to the subways and home, to tell friends that they "had seen the Babe." It was weeks before Fresh Meadow even looked like a golf course again. The fund prospered but the greenskeeper at Fresh Meadow hasn't been the same man since.

Ruth's charm and appeal were catholic. When he trained in St. Petersburg with the Yankees, elderly ladies from Iowa would edge timidly up to him for his autograph. It was probably the first time they had even seen a man in a baseball uniform. They didn't know about baseball, but they knew about Ruth.

One spring in Florida Babe drove his big car to a service station for gas. A town car with liveried chauffeur came into the filling station while the tank in Babe's car was being connected with the pump. An elderly, dowager-type woman in the back seat, who could have been the widow of the Late George Apley, gazed with interest at Ruth and his car and finally felt impelled to say something, although it probably was the first time in her life she ever spoke to a stranger without being formally introduced.

"Pardon me, Mr. Ruth," said this Victorian, "but I see you have a new car. Are the brakes on it hydraulic or mechanical?"

Ruth was equally elegant in his response. He knew class when he saw it and he decided the dame was entitled to an exhibition of his linguistic skill.

"Really, Madam," purred the Babe, delicately picking his teeth, "I haven't the faintest consumption."

Marshall Hunt, a sports writer who was with him at the time, told him he should have said "conception" but Babe arched an eyebrow at him, implying that he knew when he was being kidded.

In recent years crowds of celebrity hunters have thronged airports, railroad terminals and stage doors for a glimpse of crooners or movie stars. Frank Sinatra and Van Johnson are two young men who seem to affect 'teen-agers most curiously. Yet the adulation of Ruth was spontaneous. There were no press agents in the background, to move Machiavelli-like and maneuver mass-swoonings among the bobby-soxers.

The crowds which followed Babe materialized by accident and followed him by design, instead of vice versa. Ruth never deliberately attracted attention, yet baseball has never come close to his equal as a gate attraction. The tinsel crown of public acclaim was thrust upon him. And, come to think of it, he wore it pretty well.

3

The First Home Run

There weren't many people in the stands at the Polo Grounds that Thursday afternoon in the spring of 1915. There never were many people in the stands those days when the Yankees played. Frank Farrell had finally given up on the club after it had finished sixth the year before, but the fans had given up long before Farrell. The two Colonels, Jacob Ruppert and Tillinghast L'Hommidieu Huston, had just thrust tentative feet into the water of American League ownership and found it exceedingly cold.

Wild Bill Donovan sent Jack Warhop to the mound for the Yankees and the veteran right-hander faced a Red Sox rookie, Babe Ruth, a southpaw. Ruth had attracted some mention by being used as a starter by Rough Carrigan, although he was still moist behind the ears.

The first two innings were runless and Ruth was the first hitter for the Sox in the top half of the third. Warhop made one a little too good for the busher and he belted it into the upper right field stands. He drew a polite patter of applause from the scattering of fans as he pigeon-toed his way around the bases, but certainly nobody in the stands, or in either dugout, realized that history was being enacted before their eyes, that baseball, as they had known it up until then, was being ushered out and that a new era of prosperity and home runs was on the threshold.

Keystone

All was serene when John J. McGraw and the Babe shook hands before the first subway series at the Polo Grounds in 1921. The Giant manager, however, soon became irked because Ruth and the Yankees were outdrawing his own Giants and chased his tenants from the Polo Grounds. The result was Yankee Stadium, baseball's biggest plant, and greater crowds than ever for the American Leaguers.

This was Ruth's first major league home run and it was an ironic quirk that it was delivered against a club for which Babe was to hit so many home runs later. And it was prophetic that it should be hit at the Polo Grounds, where Ruth was later to play for three seasons as a Yankee hero, to the rage and envy of John McGraw. As a matter of fact, McGraw's indignation at Babe Ruth, at the tenant Yankee club as a whole for outshining his own Giants, eventually drove him to evict the Yankees, a boomerang which hurt the National League grievously and gave the American League an ascendancy which it has never surrendered. The two Colonels crossed the turgid Harlem and built their own ball park, Yankee Stadium, within plain sight of the

Polo Grounds. It was Ruth's home runs which built this park and it was the first of these homers that he stroked that afternoon of May 6, 1915.

This home run of Ruth's made no headlines the next day, although it did elicit some slight comment. It was, after all, only the second home run Babe had hit in professional baseball. The year before he had hit one for Providence, while playing in Toronto on September 5, a homer which was somewhat obscured by his pitching feats that afternoon when he shut out the Leafs 9 to 0, with one hit.

It would be nice to record that Ruth's homer enabled him to win his pitching duel with Warhop, but it didn't happen that way. The Babe and Jack hooked up in a tight, close battle but Doc Cook singled for the Yankees in the thirteenth to send Hughie High home with the run which beat the Red Sox, 4 to 3.

An anonymous historian, chronicling the game for the New York *Times* devoted as many words to Ruth's pitching as he did to his home run, reporting:

> For Boston, the big left-handed pitcher, Babe Ruth, was all that a pitcher was supposed to be and more. He put his team into the running with a home run rap into the upper tier in right field. . . . First up in the third, with no apparent effort, he slammed a home run into the stands.

It is well to note that Ruth's first major league home run was hit into the *upper* stands at the Polo Grounds. Babe's greatness was not only that he hit so many home runs, but that he hit them so far. The big fellow didn't just hit home runs over the fence—commendable as that is—he hit them over the roof.

Anybody who saw Ruth play more than a few times has a distinct recollection of at least one spectacular home run the Babe tied into. A clout Ruth hit in Tampa in a spring exhibition game against the Giants in 1919 generally gets the nod as being the longest ever fashioned by the great man, but there is no way of proving that it actually was. This one happened to catch the eye of the many New York writers covering the game and some of them had the enterprise to go out and measure it afterward.

Columbia George Smith was the victim of Ruth's drive that day at the old Tampa fairgrounds, which later came to be known as Plant

Brown Bros.

The Babe as the Red Sox home run king when he astonished the baseball world by clouting twenty-nine homers in the 1919 season.

Field. Babe hit the ball to right center and it not only went well beyond the outfielders but cleared a race track which circled the playing field. Fred Lieb, Frank Graham and Paul Shannon were among the group who put a tape measure to the drive after the game and found it had traveled over 500 feet. Since 350 feet is a home run of creditable proportions and a 400-footer is a breath-taker, you can imagine the stir created by this Homeric (pun) hit.

There are three or four homers among the many I've seen Babe hit which I remember with especial clarity. One was in the sixth game of the 1923 World Series against the Giants at the Polo Grounds, a drive which cleared the roof in right field, just where it starts to curve toward center, and landed in a lot outside the park among a group of astonished West Indians who were playing cricket. He hit this off Art Nehf, the lion-hearted left-hander, in the first inning and the doughty Nehf went on to blank the Yanks for the next six rounds until the roof fell in on him in the eighth and the Yanks won their first World Series. Nine years later, at Wrigley Field, Chicago, I saw him blast the much-discussed "called shot" home run against Charley Root, but that drive will be treated later on.

One home run record which eluded the Babe for a long time, although it had been achieved by many other ball players who had no great reputations as sluggers, was that of hitting three home runs in one game. It was in the first game of a double header against the Athletics at Shibe Park on May 21, 1930, that the big fellow finally turned the hat trick and the third of his homers was a really spectacular drive.

The press box in Shibe Park is up in the third deck, so steep an ascent that the less rugged among the Philadelphia baseball writers suffer from chronic nosebleeds and there was talk, before the elevator was installed, of replacing the ushers with St. Bernards.

Although the players look something like pygmies from this eagle's aerie, it affords a dandy view of the streets beyond the ball park and the outlying precincts of North Philadelphia, including the railroad station. The right field wall is about ten feet high and, until the management erected a canvas barrier, enterprising owners of the two-story-and-basement red brick flats across the street built knockdown bleachers on their rooftops and did a fine business at fifty cents a head. This was when the A's were winning pennants. When they dropped back into the cellar, no self-respecting Philadelphian would think of sitting on a roof to watch the Athletics.

This, however, was in 1930 when the A's were leading the league. Their World Series triumph over the Cubs in 1929 was like a heady wine to the fans and they were out in force at Shibe Park that balmy May afternoon to hoot at the once-haughty Yankees, now stumbling through their first season after the death of Miller Huggins. But there was no hooting of Babe in this particular game for, after hitting two man-sized homers, he really put the wood to the third one.

The drive not only cleared the fence, it soared past the street beyond the fence, the rooftop with its improvised bleachers, the backyard of that house, the adjoining backyard of a house on the next block, landed on the roof of the second house and bounded into the street, two blocks from the ball park!

Navin Field in Detroit, now Briggs Stadium, also has a lofty press perch but an elevator was installed there early, the first in any ball park. Like the press box at Shibe Park, this perch used to afford a view of the streets beyond the park until the right field stands were double-decked almost all the way around to center.

One sunny Sunday afternoon there in 1929, I watched the flight of one of Ruth's homers which, for total mileage, must have been the longest of all Babe's homers, although it didn't travel as far on the fly as some that he hit.

One of the streets beyond the ball park comes in at a right angle to the fence, parallel to the right field foul line. It is, of course, a paved street. The ball Babe hit this particular day cleared the bleachers with something to spare, struck the asphalt in the middle of the street and took off out of sight in a series of long bounds, much like a frightened kangaroo. There was a group of kids gathered on the corner and one of them mounted his bicycle and pedaled furiously after the ball. After what seemed like five minutes, I saw the boy return at a much more leisurely pace, triumphantly exhibiting his trophy of the chase to his playmates.

In the spring of 1926, Ruth hit a home run at the Smokies' park in Knoxville which, like the blast against the Giants in Tampa, added nothing to his record but is still remembered by all who saw it. This was when the Yankees and Dodgers used to barnstorm all the way home from Florida together, with the Yankees usually belting the

Keystone

Another milestone for the Big Fellow! Babe crossing the plate at Navin Field, Detroit, July 13, 1934, after hitting his 700th home run. He paid the kid who found the ball twenty dollars for returning it to him.

daylights out of the Dodgers during the afternoon on the ball field and the Dodgers cleaning up the Yankees in poker games at night on the Pullmans. That particular spring the exhibition series was remarkable for the fact that the Dodgers didn't win a single ball game all the way from Florida to Yankee Stadium.

Behind the left field fence in Knoxville was a tall, gaunt tree, devoid of foliage but blooming with youngsters who wanted to see the ball game. Dazzy Vance was pitching for Brooklyn and in the first inning Ruth tied into one. The ball whistled toward left field, over the fence and through the tree, with the result that kids were tumbling from the limbs for the next five minutes! For distance, this didn't compare with the majority of the big fellow's homers, but for laughs it was one of his best.

One thing which I always expected Babe to do, but, which he never did, was to get a home run on a pop fly. It may sound ridiculous unless you've seen the altitude of some of the Ruthian pop-ups. I frequently saw him get two-baggers on them and he did get an inside-the-park homer on a pop fly to the outfield, but since the ball landed some 300 feet from home plate it could hardly be considered a pop-up. This homer, hit against the Red Sox at Yankee Stadium, fell behind the outfielder, but was so lofty that Babe was at third when it reached the ground.

Ruth's pop-ups, like everything else about the man, were majestic. They gained such altitude that infielders used to stagger waiting for them to come down. The Babe, in his younger days, would sprint on these pop flies and often would be perched on second by the time the infielder "gave up on the ball," as the ball players' phrase has it. Infielders, with their heads thrown back and staring at a blank sky for several seconds, frequently succumb to temporary vertigo or lose the ball in the sun.

When Ted Williams sought to confound the infield shift the Cardinals employed against him in the 1946 World Series by placing a bunt down the third base line, there were many Red Sox fans at Fenway Park who thought their hero had displayed unusual ingenuity. Their memories were short, for Ruth was an extremely skillful bunter.

Naturally, Babe didn't bunt very often, but he laid down enough bunts to keep infielders from playing him too deep and he hit to the opposite field often enough to discourage over-shifting. Opposing ball clubs played Ruth to the right, as they might be expected to play any left-handed pull hitter, but they never went to the extremes used against Williams in 1946, nor even the modified shifts previously employed in the National League against dead pull hitters like Cy Williams or Wally Berger.

When Ruth first came to the Yankees and concentrated on the inviting right field wall of the Polo Grounds, a couple of American League clubs not only shifted on him but played the second baseman in short right field. The big fellow dragged a ball or two past the pitcher's box for base hits and the second baseman soon came into the infield proper.

There was no questioning Babe's power to the opposite field. The home run he hit off Vance in Knoxville, which chased the kibitzing kids from the tree top, was hit to the opposite field and it had as much carry to it as a well-hit iron shot in golf. In 1929 Ruth went all through the Florida exhibition games without getting a single homer, but he hit a ball against the left field bleacher wall in Dallas on the barnstorming trip north, a drive which must have carried 400 feet on a line.

Moe Berg, the erudite Princetonian, can talk baseball in a dozen different languages. Berg, who came to the Dodgers in 1923 as a shortstop, eventually became a catcher, then a coach and stayed in baseball almost twenty years until he entered the Office of Strategic Services immediately after Pearl Harbor. Moe was a keen student of baseball and he unhesitatingly calls Ruth the greatest hitter he ever watched.

"There have been only a few ball players who were able to impress other ball players as Ruth did," declared Berg. "When the big guy came to the plate in batting practice ball players on both clubs stopped whatever they were doing to watch him hit.

"I don't know whether the Babe paid any attention to the count against him or not, but I do know that he is the only ball player I ever saw, with the possible exception of Rogers Hornsby, who didn't shorten up when the pitcher had two strikes on him.

"Jimmy Foxx, Hank Greenberg, Ted Williams, Joe DiMaggio, Lou Gehrig, all of the great hitters I've seen, took precautions with two strikes, but not the Babe. Either consciously or unconsciously the others would choke their grip on the bat a bit or shorten their swing, concentrating to get a piece of the ball. Ruth never held back with two strikes. He took his full cut, just as if it were the first pitch to him."

Veteran baseball men, players, managers, scouts and executives, are unanimous in the opinion that there never was a ball player who could pull the club head through the ball like Ruth. His timing was flawless, with his wrists snapping into the swing at the precise split-second of contact with the ball. The Babe used to "take ball games right out of the catcher's glove," as the players say.

Although Ruth tried to pull every ball, his power was such that none but the brave, or foolhardy, tried to pitch outside to him. The Babe could pull an outside pitch directly through the pitcher's box and none of the flingers cared to risk life or limb by having line drives from his bat whistle about their ears. It was physically safer to pitch inside to Ruth and just hope and pray that he didn't pull the ball into the stands. Or over them.

Ruth maintained his home run power right up to the end of his playing days. Only a week before he quit the Braves in 1935, the Babe hit three home runs in succession at Forbes Field, Pittsburgh, the most difficult park for homers by a left-handed batter. One of these drives went over the roof of the right field grandstand, the only ball ever hit over that roof.

Three home runs in one game is quite an unusual performance. Ruth did it only twice in his career, the other time being five years earlier in Shibe Park. But the Babe, of course, had to wind things up with a flourish. His last major league home runs were not only three in one game, but were hit in succession and one of them was the longest drive in the history of baseball in Pittsburgh. And Babe then was fat, forty and out of shape.

Between that blast into the upper deck at the Polo Grounds off Jack Warhop twenty years before and the one which cleared the right field roof of Forbes Field, Ruth had hit 712 other home runs in championship games, a grand total of 714 homers, a record which is likely to stand for many years, perhaps forever. There is no player in the game today who has a chance of matching Ruth's total bag of home runs. His other records, including the sixty he hit in the season of 1927, may be eclipsed, but in total homers the big fellow stands alone.

Ruth's 714 home runs do not take into consideration the fifteen he delivered in World Series competition, nor the one he hit in the first All-Star game ever played, at Comiskey Park in 1933. There is, of course, no tabulation of the many home runs the Babe blasted in barnstorming trips, all the way from Florida to Tokyo. It is quite possible that the man unloaded a thousand home runs in the two decades between the one against Warhop in the Polo Grounds and the one against Guy Bush in Pittsburgh!

Seven years after he was through, Ruth came back to the Yankee Stadium in 1942 to bat against Walter Johnson. Ed Barrow, then president of the Yankees, brought the pair together as an added attraction to a Sunday double header for the purpose of raising funds for a war time relief agency.

Wide World

Back for one last fling. Walter Johnson, Benny Bengough, Billy Evans and Ruth before the Babe staged his home run exhibition for the Army-Navy Relief Fund at Yankee Stadium, August 23, 1942. It was the last time Babe wore a Yankee uniform.

Ruth was to bat against Johnson between games, with Benny Bengough catching and Billy Evans umpiring. When the quartet took their places, the players of both teams lined the dugout steps, as interested and as tense as any fan in the stands.

The Big Train couldn't get the first few pitches across but he finally got one over and Babe lined it into the right field stands for a home run, some 295 feet away. Johnson continued to pitch and Ruth continued to bat. He fouled off a couple, raised one of those tremendous pop flies in the vicinity of second base and, finally, on Johnson's twentieth pitch, the big fellow really caught hold of one.

The ball sped toward the third tier of the Stadium in right field, a sector where home runs are rarely hit. The drive was hooked too much, so that when it finally landed in the upper deck it was foul by a foot or so, but Babe, with his inherent sense of the dramatic, tossed away his bat and minced around the bases exactly as if it were a bona fide home run.

Fair or foul, it was a tremendous drive and the Yankees, some of whom had never seen the man whose home runs built the ball park which housed them, were as generous in applauding the fat man as the fans themselves.

Back in the clubhouse, Barrow stopped around to thank the boys personally for their cooperation. He shook hands with Walter first and then stepped over by the stool where Babe was undressing.

"Thanks for helping out, Babe," said Barrow, extending his hand.

"Thanks for asking me, Ed," replied Babe, shaking hands. "It's nice to be back—even for a day."

It was the last time anybody ever saw Ruth in a Yankee uniform and those who were there will remember that the big fellow hit a ball into the top deck.

4

The Big Decision

In the course of over half a century in baseball, Edward Grant Barrow accumulated almost as many relics, mementoes and souvenirs of the national pastime as are to be found in the game's shrine at Cooperstown, New York. One, which he apparently esteemed above all others since it was never very far from his person, was a framed photograph of himself seated at a desk, surrounded by three other persons. It was taken in the Boston office of the Red Sox in January, 1918, the year Barrow succeeded Jack Barry as manager of the Sox.

The photo, to Barrow's mind, depicts a truly historic occasion. With Ed in the group are Harry Frazee, the theatrical promoter who was president of the Red Sox, Babe Ruth and Stuffy McInnis. The ceremony was the signing of Babe and Stuffy to Red Sox contracts for 1918 and it probably was the last time that any other ball player was thus teamed up with Babe. In later years, the signing of Ruth came to be an event which received only slightly less newspaper and newsreel coverage than the inauguration of a president of the United States.

To any Boston fan who studies the picture, it has an even more lasting significance. In later years Frazee came to enjoy the same social standing in New England's cultural center as General Gage held in that period when liberty was still in its cradle. Frazee was so hopelessly involved in business debts outside of baseball that he eventually sold every able-bodied person wearing a Red Sox uniform and practically all of them to the Yankees. All the king's horses and all the king's men couldn't put Boston baseball together again until Tom Yawkey's checkbook and Ted Williams' bat finally turned the tide nearly three decades later.

The Sporting News

Ed Barrow (left), Ruth, Stuffy McInnis and Harry Frazee in the Red Sox office in January, 1918. Frazee had just purchased McInnis, first baseman of Connie Mack's $100,000 infield.

The presence of McInnis in this photograph is interesting because Stuffy represented the high tide of American League baseball in Boston under Frazee. The dark-haired little Irishman was a ball player whom Frazee bought, instead of selling. Outside of Harry's friends and relatives, there are few who can recall that there was a time when Harry was buying ballplayers for the Red Sox.

Whether Barrow cherished this picture as unique proof that Frazee once added ball players to the Red Sox roster, he never said. It is quite possible that that angle gave Ed an occasional dry chuckle, but it is more likely he retained the photograph through the years as a reminder of his first direct contact with Ruth, an association which eventually was to change baseball more than any other single factor.

"Ruth was a tall slim fellow in those days," recalled Barrow. "His face was round and mooney, but his body hadn't started to fill out."

When the photographers had expended their flash powder and departed, Barrow gave the Sox secretary, Larry Graber, a five-dollar bill and told him to take Ruth and McInnis to the nearby Boston Tavern and buy them lunch, this being in an era when a five-dollar bill went a long way.

An hour or so later the secretary returned with the somewhat incredulous look later attributed to the observers at the Bikini atom bomb tests. Graber was obviously a shaken man as he reported to the new manager of the Red Sox.

"You owe me two dollars, Ed," he said. "The check for lunch was seven dollars."

"What?" roared Barrow, in tones which later were to become familiar to road secretaries, league presidents, managers and countless generations of ball players and baseball writers.

"Ed," said Graber in the awed tones of a man who hardly expects to be believed, "did you ever see that big guy eat? He had a whole custard pie for dessert!"

Ruth, even in those days, had other distinctions to recommend him besides an enormous appetite. He was a great left-handed pitcher, great in an era of great pitching, the best the major leagues had ever enjoyed before or since. In his two previous seasons with Boston, Babe had won a total of forty-six games, twenty-three each year, and had an earned run average of 1.75 per nine-inning game for 1916, when the Sox won a pennant and a World's Championship, and a mark of 2.02 for 1917, when Boston finished second.

Barry, the 1917 manager, and Bill Carrigan before him had used Ruth in the outfield and as a pinch hitter but rather sparingly. The Babe was a remarkable batter even then, but he hadn't yet achieved his amazing knack of pulling the club-head through the ball to produce home runs. His total number of home runs, after three full

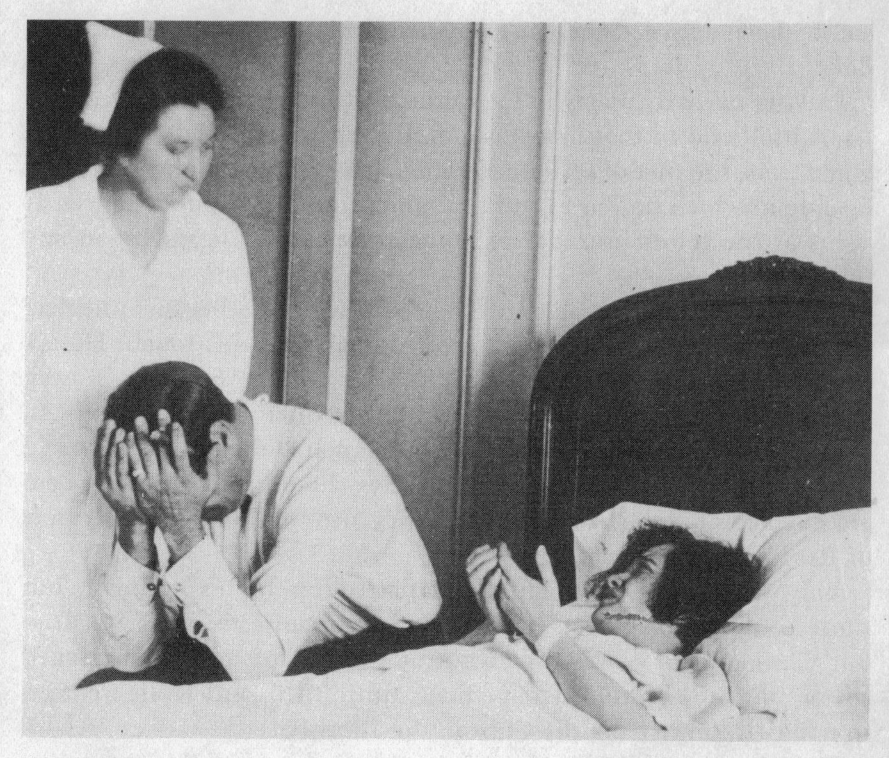

Acme

The Babe and his first wife had a turbulent marital career, punctuated by separations and reconciliations, one of the latter being this scene in a Boston hospital in 1924.

seasons in the American League was a meager nine. He was later to hit that many in a week.

Recognizing the latent talent of Ruth, Barrow took him aside one day in 1918 and asked him if there were any reason why he couldn't take his turn on the mound every fourth day and play the outfield on other days. Ed had gone a little further than the other managers with Babe and had delved into his personality. He knew that Ruth loved to hit, knew in advance that the big fellow would be agreeable. This was but the first of many excursions and explorations Barrow was to make into Ruth's soul, many of them with surprising results. The late Sigmund Freud probably would have rewritten many of his tomes had he been afforded the same opportunities for psychoanalyzing the Babe.

Playing more regularly in the outfield, Ruth's true genius began to assert itself and in that first season under Barrow the Babe hit eleven home runs, the first of seventeen consecutive seasons in the American League in which he was to run his homer total into double figures. It also was the fewest number of home runs he ever again hit in any full season.

As Ruth became an outfielder and a slugger, he began to neglect his pitching talents, although he never really lost his touch. He appeared in only twenty games as a pitcher for the Sox that season, winning thirteen. Babe pitched even less frequently the next season, because by then Barrow was riding his hunch and riding it hard.

When Barrow first decided that the Sox should have the daily benefit of Babe's bat, he had hoped that they also would have the services of Ruth's stout left arm.

Barrow thought he might be criticized for his experiment, but there couldn't have been much criticism because the Red Sox beat out Cleveland to win the pennant at the end of the war-shortened season of 1918, Boston's last pennant until 1946, and Ruth went on to win two games from the Cubs in the World Series.

That Barrow radically altered the national pastime by converting Ruth into an outfielder goes without saying. Nor can it be brushed off by assuming that if Barrow hadn't made the switch some other manager would have, for Ruth already had played under two Boston managers, neither of whom was willing to sacrifice the Babe's great pitching skill for his daily batting power.

When Babe's big bat began to boom home runs in American League parks, baseball came to the end of one era and the beginning of another. His home runs forced a change in baseball strategy as radical as that caused in football by the introduction of the forward pass. Just as aerial football outmoded the grinding out of yards and opened the game to new and broader vistas, so did the home run affect baseball.

It became obvious that playing for one run was passé when the big fellow with one swish of the bat could cancel out all that had gone before, could negate all the petty scheming, the bunting, the base stealing. The home run, like the lethal knockout punch of Jack

Dempsey and Joe Louis, was the broad, direct approach to victory, the short cut so esteemed by Americans in sport and in business, in recreation and in war.

After being sold to the Yankees, with the inviting short barrier of the Polo Grounds to shoot at, Ruth really scaled the heights. When he hit twenty-nine home runs in his final year with the Red Sox, 1919, that was supposed to be the *ultima Thule* of slugging. It was doubted that anybody ever again, even Ruth, would amass that many home runs in one year. In his first season with the Yankees, as Babe was spraying home runs all over the landscape to reach the astounding total of fifty-four, baseball was rocked by the sole major scandal in its history.

Just as the 1920 season was drawing to a close, it leaked out that several members of the Chicago White Sox had lent open ears, and open hands, to professional gamblers to throw the 1919 World Series to Cincinnati. The evidence was irrefutable and the bribe-takers were barred from baseball for life, their records in many cases stricken from the books.

The punishment, absolute as it was, undoubtedly served as a warning to any other players who might be taken to a mountain top and shown the cities of the world, but it didn't restore public confidence in the game. Baseball could survive many things—bad management, maladministration, disregard of the clientele—but it couldn't withstand public skepticism, cynicism or indifference. And it was only because Ruth was hitting home runs in undreamed of profusion that the public didn't turn sour on baseball then and there.

Baseball is a game as peculiarly American as the hot fudge sundae. People who wouldn't be found dead at a civic betterment meeting take a fierce local pride in a victory by the home team, despite the fact that the home team, in most instances, contains neither natives nor residents of the community which it represents. Two close friends of mine were shot and killed for slurring the Dodgers by a young man who had never seen any of the Dodgers face to face. The sale of a popular ball player can arouse more public ire in any municipality than the discovery that a hitherto respected political figure made a huge fortune selling rusty sewer pipes to the city, to the consequent detriment of that city's financial and sanitary standing. In Washington, the nation's capital, there was more conversation in 1924 over the

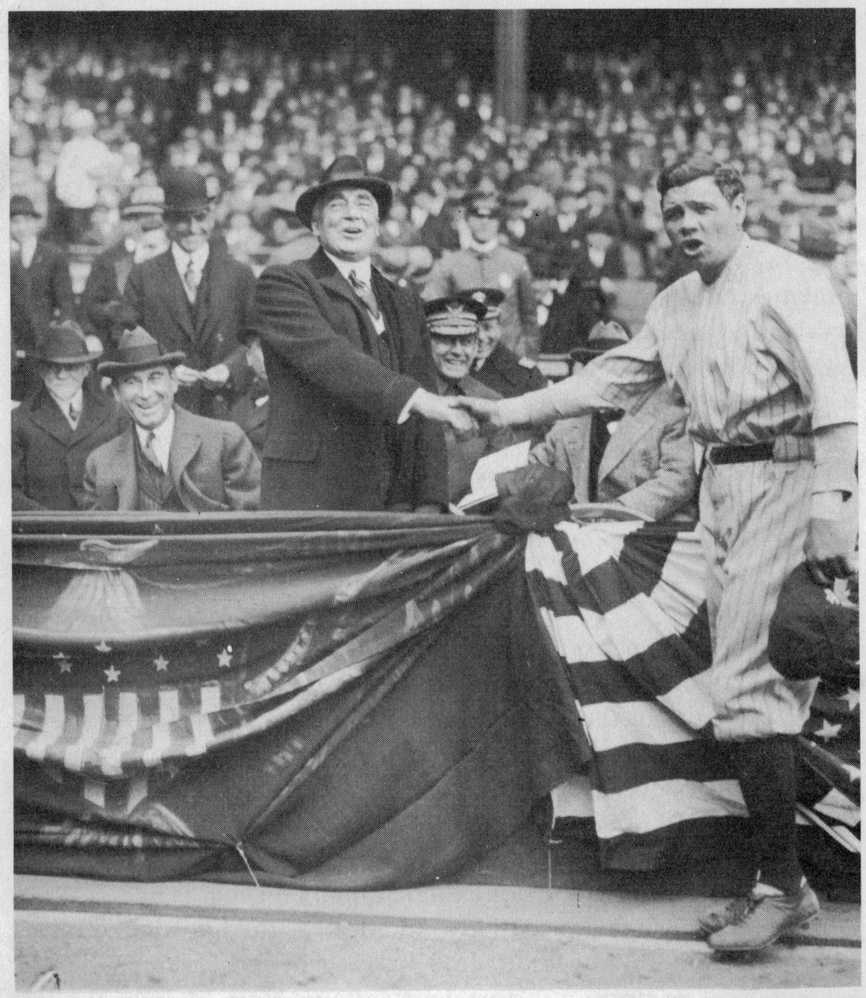

International

President Warren G. Harding, who once owned a ball club, shakes hands with Ruth before a Yankee-Senator season opener in Washington.

first pennant and World's Championship of the Senators than over the scandals of the Harding administration, then shrieking and reeking from the front pages of the newspapers. Speculation over the manner and reason for the sudden death of a president of the United States was more restrained than speculation over Bucky Harris' choice of pitchers for the World Series with the Giants.

Because the fan chooses to regard baseball as a public utility rather than a private enterprise there is no telling what might have happened to the game if Ruth hadn't come along with his home runs at a time when a great many fans felt they had been betrayed. Baseball conceivably could have weathered the storm of public disapproval without Babe's flamboyant belting, but this is highly debatable. The question of what would have happened to baseball without Ruth is purely academic, for the Babe was there and his deeds of derring-do at the plate shared the headlines with the perfidy of the Black Sox.

Baseball owners, by and large, are a much abused lot. Not many of them have the qualifications to be asked to guest-star on the radio program, Information Please. Indeed there are some who would be more at home on another ethereal quiz show, It Pays to be Ignorant. Nevertheless, even the densest of the magnates saw in Ruth's home runs the perfect anodyne for the reverberations which followed the revelations in the Federal Court in Cook County, Illinois.

With a singular unanimity in a breed so highly individualistic, the executives rallied under the banner of swat. If home runs were what the public wanted, home runs were what the public would get. The ball mysteriously gained in resiliency. Players who considered it a moral victory to reach an outfielder with a fly ball were now hitting fly balls not only over the heads of the outfielders but into the stands behind them. The home run gold rush was on. In 1921, Ruth's second year as a Yankee, there were more home runs hit in the major leagues than in any three seasons previous to 1920 and the homer total has risen steadily ever since, with the exception of the last two seasons during World War II.

With straight face and solemn mien, it was explained that the first World War had resulted in a scarcity of Australian yarn, that the machines which bound the yarn around the inner core of the baseball were improved to the point where the yarn was being wound more tightly. But actually, they said, the balls were no more lively than those used in the past. The owners shied away from charges of stimulation as though they were members of The Jockey Club.

It wasn't entirely the lively ball which led to the increased home run production. Legislation was introduced to deprive pitchers of whatever advantages they still retained over the batter. The spitball, the emery ball and the shine ball and all allied freak deliveries were banned. Umpires were instructed to put a new ball into play any time the one in use became scuffed or soiled, thus assuring the hitter of a shiny white target at all times.

With all these factors in their favor the hitters went out and did something for themselves. Ruth's salary already had started to approach that of the president, so the scientific hitters decided to become second Ruths and grab themselves a ladleful of the gravy which had become so suddenly plentiful. The choke hitter all but disappeared from baseball, as the quondam weak sisters gripped the bat at the farthermost reaches of the handle and began swinging for the fences, *à la* Babe.

Thus did Ruth, in the span of two or three seasons after he had been switched to an outfielder by Barrow, not only save baseball its place in the affections of the public, but radically alter the entire conception of the game. Babe's home runs, even to this day, remain the greatest single influence on the game in its entire history. Attendance, profits and salaries skyrocketed, new and grander stadiums were built, old ones were improved and modernized. And it all traced back to Barrow's decision to play Babe seven days a week, instead of pitching him every fourth day, a decision for which Ed feared he might be criticized.

Barrow had a high regard for Ruth's pitching ability and he reached the decision only after carefully weighing Babe's divided talents, one against the other.

"The Babe was as good a left-handed pitcher as I ever saw," declared Barrow one day. "He had everything—speed, control and a good breaking ball. He didn't care whom he pitched against, and half the time didn't even know.

"When the Red Sox won the pennant in 1918 I went over the Chicago hitters with our club before the first game of the World Series. The Cubs had an outfielder named Leslie Mann, who might hit a long ball and cause you trouble or cost you a ball game. On the other hand you could impair his efficiency by pitching tight to him and driving him away from the plate.

"I told my pitchers this, stressing the fact that it might be a good idea to loosen Mann up early in the first game of the Series, so that he'd carry that mental hazard with him every time he came to bat.

"Mann was a right-handed batter, a husky chap with a peculiar build. In fact, John McGraw used to call him 'The Centaur,' a man's head on a horse's body. There was another outfielder playing with the Cubs at the time, a little chunky fellow with blond hair, Max Flack, a left-handed hitter.

"The first time Ruth pitched against Flack he cut loose with one that clipped Max squarely on the forehead. Fortunately, it didn't hurt him and when the inning was over, Babe came back to the bench all smiles.

" 'Well, manager,' he said to me, 'I guess I loosened up that Mann guy all right.' He was the most surprised fellow in the ball park when he learned he had been pitching to Flack instead of Mann."

When Ruth was confined to a Manhattan hospital early in 1947, several writers at different times attempted to draw Barrow out on the subject of Ruth, specifically on the subject of the day in the Red Sox clubhouse when Barrow, some twenty years Ruth's senior but a bull of a man nevertheless, removed his coat and offered to have it out with the Babe then and there to prove once and for all that he, Barrow, was the manager and that Ruth was subject to his authority. Although the coat came off, the fight didn't, but Babe was fairly amenable to Ed from that day forth.

Barrow never would talk of Ruth's extra-curricular activities, even to sports writers who were intimate friends of his. He did reveal, however, that he once made an arrangement with the Babe in regard to Ruth coming in after hours. Babe, even early in his career, kept the hours of a night watchman and it would have required a confirmed insomniac to keep tabs on him. Ed determined he wasn't going to sit up the better part of the night to find out where Ruth had been, or what time he came back to the hotel.

"I'll tell you what to do, Babe," said Barrow. "Whenever you come in, no matter how late it is, drop a note in my box and tell me what time you reached the hotel. But don't lie to me."

The arrangement worked out all right, too. There was a note in

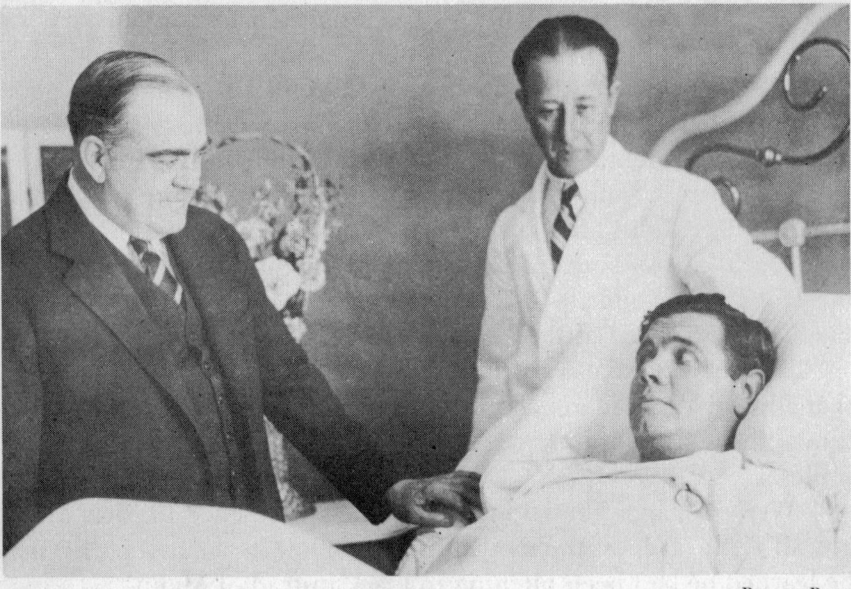

Brown Bros.

Despite their differences, contractual and otherwise, Ed Barrow always was the Babe's friend. Here he is visiting Babe in a New York hospital in 1925.

Barrow's box every morning and Babe was always truthful about reporting the time he returned. The only inconsistency was that Babe, who in those days always addressed Barrow as "Manager" in conversation, chose to make his salutation on the notes, "Dear Eddie." It is a pity Barrow never saved any of the notes, for they would have made a charming addition to American letters.

One January Sunday in 1920, Barrow received a phone call to meet Frazee in Manhattan's Hotel Knickerbocker. He went down and found his employer putting away a few drinks with the manner of a man who has bad news to impart.

"Hello, Simon," greeted Frazee. It was Harry's traditional greeting for Barrow, on the not entirely unwarranted assumption that in a business deal Ed displayed many of the less charming and more tenacious characteristics of Simon Legree.

"You're going to be sore as hell at me for what I'm going to tell you," said Frazee once the amenities had been observed.

"I've had a premonition this was coming for a long time," replied Barrow, "you're going to sell the big fellow. Well, I expected it, Harry, but let me tell you—you're going to ruin yourself and the Red Sox in Boston for a long time to come."

"There isn't any other way out," declared Frazee moodily. "They've got me up against the wall and I need money desperately. The Yankees

Keystone

A-hunting we will go! This is how the Babe looked at the time the Red Sox sold him to the Yankees.

are going to give me $100,000 for Ruth and besides that Colonel Ruppert is going to give me a personal loan of $350,000. And I can talk him and Colonel Huston out of some players, too. I'm sorry, but that's the way it is and it has to be done."

"If it has to be done, it has to be done," said Barrow philosophically, "but no players. You've made a fool out of me before by selling star ball players for cash and has-beens. Let this be a straight cash transaction and then we're not trying to kid anybody."

And, as simply as that, did Babe Ruth become a Yankee, to play a major share in the winning of seven pennants for a club which had never won one before, to help build the first great baseball stadium, and to lay a solid foundation for the most powerful dynasty the game has ever known.

Although at this time Ruth had yet to hit his first home run as a Yankee, he already was on the way up. Miller Huggins, who had just completed his second season as Yankee manager, went to California where the Babe was wintering to give him a new contract. After winning the World's Championship in 1918, Barrow had signed Ruth to a two-year contract at $10,000 a year. This still had a season to run, but Hug had permission to tear it up and offer Ruth a new one at $20,000 a year. The Babe had come a long way in the two years since he had tackled a whole custard pie for dessert in the Boston Tavern.

While Ruth was an instant success in New York with fifty-four home runs in 1920, the Yankees didn't win their first pennant until the next season when Barrow and Babe were reunited. Ed, with his star ball players being sold right and left on him by Frazee, finished fifth with the Red Sox in 1920 and began to look for greener pastures.

Colonel Ruppert, who was gradually gaining the ascendancy over Colonel Tillinghast L'Hommedieu Huston in directing the affairs of the Yankees, was a baseball fan but not baseball man. He was perfectly satisfied with Miller Huggins as manager, which was more than Huston was, but he decided that an experienced baseball man was necessary to direct the affairs of the club. Barrow had not only managed in the American League but had been president of the International League, keeping that circuit intact in the stormy days of the Federal League, when even the major leagues found it heavy sledding. So Barrow was hired to become the first general manager in baseball history.

Acme

The Babe signs a three-year contract calling for $70,000, as Ed Barrow (standing) looks on and Colonel Ruppert smiles approvingly. It was Ed who dictated Yankee policy, although the Colonel provided the checks.

Barrow continued to exert a great influence upon Ruth's career, although it is doubtful if Babe ever realized to what an extent. Now that Barrow no longer was in direct authority over him as manager, Ruth thought of Ed only as a watch-dog who sat in the Yankee offices and stood guard over the moneys of Colonels Ruppert and Huston. He no longer called Barrow "Manager" or addressed notes to him as "Dear Eddie." And whenever Babe had occasion to refer to Barrow in conversation with newspapermen he always referred to him as "Barrows." Babe's difficulty with names has become a legend but it was a new high, even for him, to make the bushy-eyebrowed Yankee executive sound like the butler in an English drawing-room comedy.

Barrow, during the decade and a half he spent with Ruth on the Yanks, was as much of a help to Babe as he had been that day in Boston when he told the Babe to discard his pitcher's toe-plate and become an outfielder. When Christy Walsh became Ruth's business manager, Babe had two shrewd men working both sides of the street for him, Walsh for Ruth himself, Barrow for Ruth and the ball club. It was Walsh who set up an annuity plan for Ruth, which paid Babe at the rate of about $12,000 a year when his baseball career was behind him.

That all of these annuities were still in force after Ruth had retired was due to the pertinacity of Walsh. Christy went to bat with Barrow to avert the cancellation of one of the policies.

During one season, Ruth signed a provisional contract. A certain sum of money was to be withheld from each pay check. If, at the end of the season, Barrow decided Ruth's behavior had been up to snuff, he was to get the money, which amounted to $5500.

When the season ended Walsh told Barrow that one of Ruth's annuity policies was in danger of being lapsed because Babe had failed to keep up the premiums. There was $3000 due and it had to be paid immediately. Christy persuaded Ed to write out a check on the Yanks for that amount.

Shortly after, Ruth visited the Yankee office to see where he stood on the matter of the withheld salary.

"Say, Ed," asked Ruth, as if he didn't know, "haven't I got some money coming to me?"

"You certainly have, Babe," replied Barrow heartily. "Twenty-five hundred dollars."

"Twenty-five hundred?" repeated Ruth. "Shouldn't it be a little more than that?"

"It would have been," smiled Barrow, "if you had kept up your payments on your annuities. I paid out $3000 the other day to keep one of your policies alive."

Ruth made one more short stab at collecting the entire jackpot. He told Barrow that he had been counting on the money because he had planned making some improvements on his farm that winter.

Barrow burst out laughing and, in a matter of seconds, Ruth joined him. The farm to which Babe was referring so grandiloquently was little more than a rockpile outside Boston. Its principal crop was boulders, which would have been ideal for Minute Men to crouch behind to take pot shots at the Redcoats, but which had little market value in current times.

When Ruth left the Yankees for his ill-fated fling with the Boston Braves in 1935, Barrow made no effort to "retire" his famed uniform, No. 3, and there were many who thought Ed was bitter about the Babe. The "3" was taken up by Twink Selkirk, Babe's immediate successor and since then has been worn by a number of Yankees, most of them remarkably undistinguished.

There never was any animosity on Barrow's part, although Babe from time to time remarked petulantly that he thought he had received rather shabby treatment from the Yankees. That there never was a place in the Yankee organization for Babe was Ruth's fault, rather than anybody else's and Barrow always has been unstinting in his praise of Ruth as a ball player.

More than once, people remarked to Barrow that in switching Ruth from a pitcher to an outfielder, he had changed the entire course of baseball.

"That's only partly true," Ed always replied. "I just put the Babe out there. He hit the home runs."

5

The Gay Life

I wonder where my Babe Ruth is tonight?
He grabbed his hat and coat and ducked from sight.
He may be at some cozy roadside inn,
Drinking tea—or maybe gin.
He may be at a dance, or may be in a fight.
I know he's with a dame,
I wonder what's her name?
I wonder where my Babe Ruth is tonight?

—*An old Baseball Writers' Song.*

The late William J. Slocum, a baseball writer who was closer to Ruth than any other member of the craft, penned the above parody in the winter of 1926. It was sung at the New York Baseball Writers' Dinner that February by Rud Rennie, a baseball writer who was closer to having an acceptable tenor voice than any other member of the craft.

The Baseball Writers' Dinner is a type of entertainment (?) and post-prandial oratory peculiar to that peculiar profession. Like its well-publicized big brother, the Gridiron Dinner in Washington, it annually lampoons and satirizes its guests, exposing the stuffing of many a shirt. The annual dinner in New York now attracts 1200 dinner-jacketed guests, who pay fifteen dollars for the privilege of sitting cheek-to-jowl in uncomfortable proximity to one another and seeing themselves ridiculously depicted on the stage by baseball writers, who, whatever their literary talents, have precious few inherited from Thespis.

These dinners are an annual affair in almost every major league city. The first was held in New York in February, 1924, with 250 guests, as an informal testimonial to Commissioner Kenesaw Mountain Landis. The speakers were John A. Heydler, National League president, an amiable and estimable gentleman but hardly a latter-day Demosthenes, and an anonymous Japanese, who spoke at some length about the undying friendship between Nippon and America, which was being perpetuated by baseball.

Since the motif of these dinners is exaggeration, it must not be assumed that the perplexity of Miller Huggins, as impersonated by Rennie, was constant as to the whereabouts of his home run hero. There were nights when Hug knew where the big fellow was. And nobody enjoyed the pungent satire of Slocum's parody at that '26 gathering more than Miller and the Babe himself, who had just survived an indefinite suspension and a $5000 fine plastered upon him by Huggins.

To understand Ruth at all, you must understand that the big fellow always did things violently, both on and off the field. Babe loved living and felt that he was as much above ordinary rules as he was above ordinary, or even extraordinary, pitching.

Baseball, to Ruth, provided a way to live and live well. When freed from the restraint and repressions imposed upon him at St. Mary's, it was only natural that he should exuberantly kick up his heels. He kicked them up so high, and so often, that it was inevitable they should go over the traces upon occasion.

Almost from the time he joined the Red Sox, Ruth had exercised his heel-kicking privilege. Duffy Lewis, who made up that immortal Sox outfield with Tris Speaker and Harry Hooper, told me that Babe once asked Manager Bill Carrigan for permission to leave the club when it had an open Sunday in Washington. This was in 1915, when it was considered not only blasphemous but also illegal to profane the Sabbath with a professional baseball game. Ruth explained to Carrigan that he wished to visit what he vaguely referred to as "my people" in nearby Baltimore. Rough gave his consent and Ruth was off, to be seen no more until the following Monday.

Lewis, now road secretary with the Boston Braves, enlightened me with the sequel to Babe's day off.

"I was walking out on the field in Washington on Monday alongside of Rough. Ruth was just ahead of us and his father, who was sitting in a box near our bench, yelled out, 'Nice going, George. You're down here and never come out to see us.'

"To this day, I can still see the scowl on Carrigan's face as he started for the Babe."

Whatever Carrigan said to the big fellow, you may be sure it made no permanent impression on Ruth. Carrigan finally resorted to doubling Ruth up on the road with Heinie Wagner, while he took an adjoining room with one of the other players.

When Ruth was purchased by the Yankees, Colonels Ruppert and Huston summoned him to a winter conference with Manager Huggins. In a manner more hurt than angry, Huston explained to Babe that his midnight excursions must stop, that he must pay strict attention to the training rules laid down by Huggins. Colonel Til, who had served with the Engineers in France, could be a pretty persuasive talker when he felt so inclined.

Ruth listened attentively to Huston's moralizing. When the Colonel was through, Babe surveyed his employers in silence. Then he exploded into what was probably the only declaration of principles he ever made.

"Look at you," barked Ruth to the astonished Huston. "Too fat and too old to have any fun. And (pointing to Colonel Ruppert) that goes for him, too!"

Huggins tried to hide a grin at this point, but was spared the trouble when Ruth jerked a contemptuous thumb in the direction of the tiny manager.

"As for that shrimp," growled the Babe, "he's half-dead right now!"

The gist of Ruth's complaint against the complainers was that he was young, lusty and vigorous. Why, therefore, should his manner of living be dictated by those who already had had their fun?

Needless to say, the two Colonels were not impressed with the logic of Ruth's plea. When he started for training camp that spring, he was accompanied by Joe Kelley, an old Oriole harking back to the glory days of Baltimore, a teammate of John McGraw and Hughie Jennings.

Wide World

Ruth was tops in the lush days of the Twenties. Here he is in the Hotel Commodore at a dinner for sports champions given by Madison Square Garden, January 15, 1928. Left to right, seated: Bill Tilden, tennis; Bobby Jones, golf; Freddy Spencer and Charley Winter, six-day bike riders. Left to right, standing: Ruth, baseball; Gene Tunney, boxing; Johnny Weismuller, swimming; Bill Cook, hockey.

Two days after the pair left for the South, Colonel Huston's phone rang at midnight. It was long distance, calling collect from Baltimore.

"Good Lord," groaned Colonel Til as he waited for the connection to be completed, "it's that blasted Ruth again. He's escaped from Kelley."

Then the booming voice of the Babe came over the phone. "Look, Colonel," said Ruth. "It's that old guy Kelley. I can't get him on the train. He met some old pals here and doesn't want to leave."

It probably marked the first time in history, certainly the first time in Ruth's personal history, that the strayed sheep had to take care of the shepherd.

Between the time Ruth and his first wife were separated and his marriage, after her death, to Clair Hodgson, a former Follies beauty, in April, 1929, the Babe was pretty much on his own. It was during this period that Ping Bodie gave such an apt description of life with Ruth that it has been used ever since by ball players who draw nocturnal prowlers as roomies.

For a time Bodie, the first of the star Italian ball players with the Yankees, and Ruth were nominal roommates.

"Who are you rooming with, Ping?" asked somebody.

"With Babe Ruth's suitcase," responded Bodie.

After Babe's second marriage, the new Mrs. Ruth made all the road trips and no Yankee manager ever again had to warble that plaintive parody, "I Wonder Where My Babe Ruth Is Tonight?"

This turn of affairs pleased nobody as much as the late Mark Roth, who served for many years as the road secretary of the Yankees. A road secretary is a combination wet nurse, father confessor and mother superior to ball players and baseball writers. It is to him they turn for light and guidance, transportation and meal money. A rugged individualist like Ruth on the squad added many additional details to what Mark, a reformed baseball writer, already considered an irksome task.

One day in the late 20's, the Yankees were playing in Chicago. Roth had taken his usual station at the pass gate and a couple of the Yankee writers, entering about fifteen minutes before game time, were surprised to hear the spiked shoes of Huggins, the mite manager, clattering up from the dark caverns of Comiskey Park to the pass gate.

"Seen the big fellow yet?" Hug anxiously asked Roth.

"Not yet," answered Mark.

"Holy cow!" ejaculated Huggins. "Where can he be? Batting practice is finished and we're taking fielding practice now. This is the end, believe me! I'm going to talk to that big ape when I catch up with him."

Just then a taxi disgorged Ruth at the entrance to the pass gate. His moon face glowing with perspiration, his coat off and carried jauntily on his little finger, the Babe brushed by with a cheery, "Hi ya, keed!" to his manager and hustled off in the direction of the Yankee dressing room.

The New York writers, witnesses to Ruth's tardy arrival, made the plodding ascent to the press box. By the time they had scaled the heights, the Yankee lineup was announced, with Babe in his outfield position and in his usual No. 3 spot in the batting order.

When the game started, Ruth was not even in sight on the Yankee bench but after the first batter flied out the Babe shot out of the dugout as though from a catapult and took the "on deck" position, kneeling some yards away from the plate while the White Sox pitcher walked the second Yankee batter.

Ruth was saluted with the usual acclaim and whacked the second pitch on a line into the seats in right field to get the Yankees off to a two-run lead. Later in the game, about the fifth or sixth inning, Ruth again toed the mark, this time with two on, and responded with his second home run of the afternoon, this one into the upper deck. The Yanks eventually won the ball game, 5 to 3, with the Babe hitting two home runs and batting in all five of the Yankee runs.

The writers who had seen Huggins anxiously scouring the horizon for Ruth before the game hustled to the Yankee clubhouse after the game to learn if any disciplinary action was to be taken. They found they had been anticipated by road-secretary Roth, who was standing alongside Hug's locker, chattering like a magpie.

Although the game had been over scarcely five minutes, Ruth burst dripping out of the shower room, toweled himself hastily and, not even pausing to comb his locks, began dressing with the celerity of a battalion chief answering a four-alarmer.

"There he is! There he is now, Hug," goaded Roth. "Are ya gonna say anything to him? Are ya, huh?"

"I should say I am going to say something to him," replied Huggins. By now Ruth had completed his hasty toilet and was virtually sprinting to the clubhouse door. Hug waved his hand at the fleeting figure of the big fellow and said, "Hi ya, Babe!"

Then Huggins spread his hands expressively in the direction of the writers and asked, "Say something to him? What the hell can you say to a guy like that?"

Midway through the season of 1924 the Yankees acquired an unusual rookie from Reading, unusual in the sense that he was well over

Keystone

Brawn and brain. The Battering Babe and the Mighty Mite, Miller Huggins, at St. Petersburg in 1927. The combination gave the Yanks their first six pennants.

thirty years of age and had been knocking around for years in the minors. He was Shags Horan, a red-faced product of St. Louis' famed Kerry Patch, a right-handed hitter who could hit a ball as far as anybody. He might have come to the majors years before except for the fact that the scouting reports on Shags indicated that he liked to take his fun where he found it and for that reason he was continuing to find it in the bushes.

Horan was no coat-toucher or celebrity-chaser, but he and Ruth clicked from the beginning like two kindred souls. The Yanks were desperately chasing Washington in an effort to win their fourth straight American League pennant, but they couldn't quite make it, falling short by two and a half games.

If anything, Shags was a realist. He knew he had been called up by the Yankees only because it was a dire emergency and that once the emergency ceased, he would be on his way again. For that reason he took his promotion in stride, making no effort to alter the habits of years. He hit an occasional long ball for the Yankees when called upon to pinch hit but did nothing spectacular. On the field anyway.

Back in the Yankee folklore is a tall tale that one night when the club was making the trip from Detroit to Cleveland by boat, the Babe and Shags thought it would be a perfectly ducky idea to dunk Manager Huggins into the waters of Lake Erie. They set out in search of him, but fortunately he could not be found. Legend or not, it is a matter of fact and record that the Yankees never again made the trip from Detroit to Cleveland by boat until the war, when the Office of Defense Transportation curtailed rail travel.

It was the following year, after Horan had gone back to the minors, that Ruth really scaled the heights or plumbed the depths, depending upon your view of revelry by night. In 1925, Babe was, for the only time in his career as an active ball player, literally unmanageable. Stricken ill on the way north from St. Petersburg, Ruth played less than 100 games, not getting into action until June, and the club fell apart without him.

Their pennant skein having been broken the year before and forced to play the first six weeks without the big fellow, too many other Yankees besides Ruth also looked upon 1925 as a wasted season. The veterans who had won three straight pennants were beginning to come apart at the seams and the replacements had not yet arrived. The club finished seventh, its only second division finish while Ruth was a member.

A salesman with a heart of gold and a purse to match showed up on one of the Yankee western trips that summer. He was affability itself, this agreeable Mr. Kelly, and nothing was too good for his baseball idols. He even located a brewery where real beer, as rare as penicillin in those needle-beer days of prohibition, might be obtained. He thought he'd like a flashlight picture of the group, just as a souvenir of the happy times he spent with his heroes. The players accompanying him to the brewery assented readily. After all, nothing was too good for Mr. Kelly, either.

It was only when they returned from this trip that Ruth and other members of the Yankees discovered that the affable Mr. Kelly was not all wool and a yard wide. He wasn't even Mr. Kelly but a private eye, a fink. Or, as Colonel Ruppert more elegantly phrased it, a special investigator. The flashlight photo from the brewery, complete with a set of "Mr. Kelly's" notes, reposed on Ruppert's desk.

Neither the pictoral nor the printed evidence daunted Ruth. Huggins eventually did, however. He announced that he had slapped a $5000 fine on the big fellow and suspended him indefinitely. The announcement was made as the Yankees were leaving St. Louis and it threw the Babe into a towering rage. He ranted to newspapermen that the fine wouldn't stick, that "When I see Jake and Barrow, we'll see where Huggins stands," etc. He was going to Chicago to see Landis, but the Yanks went there without him.

When he got to New York, Ruth found out exactly where Huggins stood. It was aces high, with both Ruppert and Barrow. And Babe, by the time the train reached Grand Central, had relented and decided not to ask for Huggins' head but merely to ask to have his own spared. Because his huffing and puffing and bluffing had been printed in every newspaper, Ruth had to see Ruppert and Barrow.

Huggins, of course, already had communicated with Barrow by phone and big Ed told Miller that the ball club was behind him. Ruppert and Barrow were ready for Babe when he entered Colonel Jake's office in the Third Avenue brewery. He was told that the fine stuck and the suspension would remain in force until such time as Huggins saw fit to lift it. And, furthermore, Babe was told that he must apolo-

Keystone

A sight as familiar as Ruth's homers. The Babe holds the lifetime major league records for strikeouts, 1330. Here he is being fanned by Schoolboy Rowe in Detroit, July 13, 1934, the same day he hit his 700th homer.

gize immediately to Hug if he ever expected to play with the Yankees again.

This was indeed forceful support of the manager, for the Yankees, in this lugubrious season above all others, were no box office attraction without Ruth. But without Ruth it had to be until he made his peace with Huggins. And it was a meek and penitent Babe who had to admit humbly that he was wrong and that Hug was right. Ruth made public apology and was restored to the good graces of the Yankees but the $5000 fine still stood.

Ruppert and Barrow reasoned that the fine had to stand or otherwise it would be only an empty gesture and Hug's authority would be in jeopardy again. By making the fine stick, the Yankee owner and general manager not only served potent notice on Ruth that he was subject to the manager, but made it plain to the rest of the ball club that if the Babe could be so severely punished nobody on the ball club was immune.

As long as Huggins lived, Ruth never challenged his authority again. Barrow recently revealed that Colonel Ruppert returned the fine to Ruth after Huggins had died, but that the Colonel had promised Hug that fine wouldn't be rescinded and stuck to that promise as long as the little manager was alive. It was returned to Babe because he had kept his promise to obey Huggins through the years which followed the big explosion.

Ruth was learning the hard way that it does no good to challenge authority. Four years earlier, he had flouted Commissioner Landis and found the net result was somewhat equivalent to getting gay with a buzz saw. When the Yankees won their first American League pennant in 1921, largely through the efforts of the Babe, who batted .378, clouted 59 home runs and batted in 170 runs, an outside promoter approached Babe and sold him a bill of goods about a post-season barnstorming tour.

Selling Ruth a bill of goods in those days required no gift of the tongue. Babe was gullible and could be sold anything until such time as he began listening to Barrow, Christy Walsh and his second wife, Clair.

Post-season barnstorming by players participating in the World Series was then under severe restrictions, although the rules have since been relaxed. The rule then read that both teams should disband immediately after the conclusion of the Series and that the members could not participate in exhibition games, either as individuals or as a team, during the year in which the Series had been played.

While the Series was being played Ruth blandly notified Landis that he intended competing in some exhibition games. He also announced that he was taking two teammates with him, Bob Meusel and Bill Piercey. After the final game, Landis went into the Yankee dressing room at the Polo Grounds and told Ruth that defying the rule would have serious consequences.

The first exhibition game was played at Buffalo on October 16 and later the teams played at Elmira and Jamestown on their way to Scranton. Colonel Huston met the barnstormers at Scranton and broke up the tour by buying out the promoter. It developed afterward that the promoter was the only one involved to show a profit on the venture.

Some weeks later, on December 5, Commissioner Landis gave his ruling. It was the first big test of his powers and the Judge didn't duck the issue. Pointing out that the rule had been adopted ten years before, after the public had been gulled by barnstorming World Series players, and that Ruth had been fined as long ago as 1916 for a similar violation, Landis then wound up and threw the book at the culprits.

"The situation involves not merely rule violation," read the Judge's report, "but, rather, a mutinous defiance by the players intended to present the question: Which is the bigger, baseball or any individual in baseball?

"There will be an order forfeiting their share of the World Series funds and suspending them until May 20, 1922, on which date, and within ten days thereafter, they will be eligible to apply for reinstatement."

Keystone

Commissioner Kenesaw Mountain Landis assures Bob Meusel and Ruth at the New Orleans training camp in 1922 that there is nothing personal in the suspensions he slapped on them for violating the barnstorming rule the previous fall.

It cost the players exactly $3362.26 and a month's pay to defy the Commissioner. Since it also cost the Yankees about $100,000 at the gate through the absence of Babe, you may imagine the pressure which was brought to bear upon Landis in an effort to have him lift the suspension. With Ruth out of the lineup for over a month, the receipts all around the American League were clipped.

Landis gave about as much ground as the Georgia mountain after which he was named. Since they were not barred from exhibition games, Ruth and Meusel were working out with the Yankees at the New Orleans training camp the following spring. Piercey, the pitcher, had been traded to Boston. As Landis approached New Orleans on his annual spring tour of the training camps, Ruppert and Barrow came down from New York to meet him and cop one last plea. They called the New York baseball writers together.

"As a favor to me," asked Colonel Ruppert, "will you kindly lay off the Judge until we can talk to him tonight? If you get to him first he'll only repeat his stand and we'll have no chance with him."

The writers laid off and Ruppert and Barrow went to see the Judge.

Landis wouldn't cut even one day from the sentences of Ruth and Meusel. And that was the last time his authority was ever disputed by a ball player. Incidentally, the Judge had no difficulty in collecting the fines from the players, since all he did was withhold their World Series checks.

There were a couple of sequels to the suspension which bear repeating. The return of the prodigals, May 20, 1922, was a big day at the Polo Grounds, with 35,000 on hand to see Babe and Bob come back to the Yankee lineup against the St. Louis Browns. It also was the scene of what the late Sid Mercer, one of the charter members of the Baseball Writers Association of America, was fond of terming "the most public bottle breaking during the prohibition era." This is the way Mercer related the story in the New York *Journal-American*:

> Two seats were reserved in the center of the old field pressbox for Colonel Huston and his bosom pal, Jimmy Allison, New York representative of a Cincinnati paper. On the chill spring afternoons Huston and Allison had been accustomed to act as press box life savers by reporting daily with a quart of verboten spirits so they could do a bit of pouring between innings under the grandstand.

May 20 was a warm day. Huston and Allison were a bit late. They arrived during the fourth inning. Allison, a snappy dresser, carried his topcoat over his arm. In an outside pocket of the coat was the customary quart.

As they entered the press section a hush fell over the Polo Grounds. The score was tied and the Yankees had a runner on third with one out and Ruth coming to bat.

The tardy pair proceeded to their seats, nodding to friends seated in the boxes directly behind the press rows. The pitcher pawed the dirt. Ruth cocked his bat. The silence was deafening.

Just then the quart descended from Allison's pocket and struck the concrete floor of the open press box with a crash that could be heard out in the bleachers. Instantly thousands of eyes were focused on the scene of the disaster. Ruth took a called ball.

Col. Huston and Allison sat down abruptly, trying to pretend that they were in no way connected with the heap of broken glass at their feet. The Colonel tapped his foot nervously, a sign of extreme agitation with him

"You so-and-so," he hissed. "The last quart, too."

Meanwhile the customers in the boxes arose, leaned over and sniffed. The precious spirits spread over the press box floor. A scribe in the front row touched a match to the trickle to test its alcoholic content. Huston softly cursed Allison. Then Ruth hit a long fly to bring in the run and an attendant swept up the press coop debris.

The incident got more space in the papers the next day than the ball game, which the Browns won, 8 to 2, by scoring seven runs in the ninth.

Ruth probably was hurt more by the suspension than by the fine, for the Babe dearly loved to play ball. It was only a few days after the alcoholic catastrophe suffered by Colonel Huston that the big fellow almost ran smack-dab into another suspension. Playing against Washington, Ruth singled and was thrown out trying to stretch his hit. Or, at least, Umpire George Hilderbrand said he was thrown out, which amounted to the same thing. The Babe, perhaps in the hope of improving the umpire's sight, threw a handful of dust in his face.

Hilderbrand promptly decorated Babe with the Order of the Thumb and Ruth returned to the dugout in a towering rage. A fan, more valorous than discreet, gave Ruth an indecorous salute and Babe took into the stands after him.

Ruppert and Huston were appalled and Barrow was speechless. It is no mean offense in baseball to take after a cash customer, particularly with the evident desire to take said cash customer apart. The gate had been dented badly enough by Ruth's previous suspension and the bosses feared another blow where it would do the most harm, right in the old bread basket or box office.

Ban Johnson, president of the American League, made the perfect decision as far as the owners in his circuit were concerned. He decided Ruth's suspension from opening day until May 20 for his barnstorming was time enough in the baseball penalty box for one season. He fined Babe $200 and ruled that the big fellow could no longer serve as team captain, a sinecure which carried $500 with it and consisted chiefly of delivering the lineup to the plate umpire before each game. Save for one year, 1935, when Ruth had left the Yankees and an effort was being made to glamorize Lou Gehrig, the Yankees have never had a player as team captain since, those duties being handled by one of the coaches.

Ruth, during the Tumultuous Twenties, was making money as fast as he could spend it, which he considered the perfect operation of the law of supply and demand. One year he made a brief post-season vaudeville tour, being paid a fairly high salary, and was delighted to learn at the end of the engagement that it hadn't cost him any money. He had broken even.

Though Babe loved fun in its all myriad forms, he never was much of a gambler. He played poker with the other Yankees on the trains nights but the stakes never were so high as to be disproportionate for one of Ruth's income. He later concentrated on bridge, and in bridge, as in poker, Babe played for the excitement, rather than the stakes.

Only once did Ruth venture among the professional wolves and he returned completely shorn. Indeed his fate might have been worse had it not been for an adamant stand on the part of Barrow. On a winter trip to Havana, Babe tackled the form at Oriental Park and returned sadder, wiser and broke. He also was in the hole to a bookmaker for a tab which the bookie told Barrow amounted to $30,000. He asked Barrow's help to collect.

"You got all the money he had on him," said Barrow angrily, "and you'll get no more."

"You wouldn't want the newspapers to get hold of this, would you?" slyly insinuated the gambler.

"I don't give a damn whether they do or not," retorted Barrow.

And that ended that.

Keystone

Private Ruth, of the 104th Field Artillery, New York National Guard, salutes General John J. Pershing in Washington.

Because of the very impetuosity of his nature, Ruth was not a very good poker player. He had card sense above the ordinary, but invariably let his love for action supersede his judgment. He got into pots in which he had no business and stayed in them long after he should have dropped out.

Back in 1924, the Dodgers picked up a veteran catcher from the minors during the training season, Señor Miguel Angel Gonzalez, the only ball player I've ever seen with a platinum tooth. Mike had been up before, with the Giants, and he was to go on from the Dodgers to become practically a legend as coach of the Cardinals.

Gonzalez joined the Dodgers just before they hooked up with the Yankees for the barnstorming trip north. There were some good poker players on that Dodger club in 1924—Jacques Fournier, Bernie Neis, Dazzy Vance, Dutch Ruether and Ivy Olson among others. And Mike, despite his fractured English, the interpretation of which baffled Americans and Cubans alike, qualified for the first flight. In fact he was one of the seeded players who nightly ventured into the Yankee Pullmans to do battle with World's Champions.

Late one night, or rather early one morning, as the train was bumping along en route from Greensboro, North Carolina, to Charlotte, Mike returned from his joust with the Yankees. His berth was opposite mine and I noticed him remove a large wad of folding money from his trouser pocket, transfer it to his wallet and then, in the time-honored tradition of cautious and travel-hardened ball players, plant the wallet in one of his sox and the sock under his pillowcase.

Gonzalez saw me watching him and gave me a wink which needed no interpreter. He then confided an observation in that curious patois which was neither Spanish nor English, nor yet a combination of both.

"Thot Baba Root," he said, "I hopa she playa beisbol longa tima, keepa maka lotsa monay."

Everybody felt the same way, Mike.

6

The Big Tummy Ache

With the exception of a troop of soldiers on the march, there is no group of men with less knowledge of its day-to-day whereabouts than a barnstorming ball club. Like an army in motion, all the ball club knows is its ultimate destination, the home park by opening day. Every day it's a new town, a new ball park. Only the road secretary seems to have even a general idea of the itinerary.

When two ball clubs are swinging the same grass roots circuit together, the confusion is naturally doubled. So it was when the Yankees and Dodgers came north from their Florida camps in the spring of 1925. Through Georgia, Alabama, Tennessee and into the Carolinas came the wandering ball players, each day importuning Mark Roth of the Yanks or the white-mustachioed Fred Hanlon of the Dodgers for such information as the next stop and the next billet. Sometimes there'd be a rush to board the trains immediately after the conclusion of the day's game, sometimes the trains would leave at midnight and, on rare occasions, there would be an overnight stop in a hotel, with a 6 A.M. call for all hands to catch an early train so as to be in the next town by game-time.

It was an early morning hop from Knoxville to North Carolina's mountain resort, Asheville. I remember some of the high jinks on the platform at Knoxville as the Yankees and Dodgers waited for their special train to be made up. One of the Brooklyn players chased burly Jack Fournier the length of the station with a toy snake. Fournier had a psychotic dread of reptiles, not only bona fide ones, which would be understandable, but also those of papier maché. The assembled athletes rubbed sleep-rimmed eyes at the amusing antics and laughed between yawns.

The train ride itself wasn't so funny. For a good part of the 100-odd mile trip from Knoxville to Asheville, the right of way of the Southern Railway parallels the French Broad River, a swift racing, tumbling stream which, from the window of the bouncing cars, took on the appearance of a rapids. Many an athlete and his breakfast parted company en route.

Arrival at Asheville was a relief. I recall going up to the Western Union counter in the station and writing upon a telegraph form when there was a sound like a scuffle behind me. I turned in time to see Babe Ruth collapse into the arms of Steve O'Neill. Steve, later a manager at Cleveland and Detroit, was a big strapping Irishman and it is a good thing he was, for it required a man of extraordinary power to hold the big fellow. Had Steve not been there to catch Ruth when he went into his tailspin Babe would have crashed to the marble floor of the station and a fractured skull is the very least he could have escaped with.

Ruth was hustled off to a local hospital and his collapse subsequently became known, through the late W. O. McGeehan, as "The Tummy Ache Heard Round the World." It was all of that. It was very nearly the end of Babe Ruth.

Tradition has it that the Babe brought about this collapse by consuming huge quantities of hot dogs, estimated at anywhere from a dozen to eighteen at a time, the cumulative effect of which was to give him an attack of acute indigestion. Just where Ruth could acquire that many frankfurters at 7 A.M. in Knoxville or on the three-hour train ride remains an unsolved mystery.

Many of us were inclined to attribute Ruth's blackout to the jolting ride over the mountains from Knoxville. When it became known that he was to be hospitalized for an indefinite period, however, that put a different aspect on things. Despite a strict censorship on his condition, or perhaps because of it, all of the newspapermen traveling with the ball clubs knew that Babe was seriously ill.

That Ruth's ailment was more than acute indigestion was evident not only because of the length of time he spent in the Asheville hospital but because of subsequent events. When he finally was permitted to leave the hospital and come to New York, he collapsed again, just as the train bringing him home was passing through Manhattan Transfer, that since-abandoned stop in the Jersey meadows where the Pennsy trains used to change from steam to electricity.

There was no question later that it was more than hot dogs which sent Ruth reeling into the arms of O'Neill that morning in Asheville and which caused his collapse almost two weeks later as he was arriving in New York. The Babe was a sick man, seriously ill for the first time in his life. It was mirrored in all of his later actions that season, his defiance of Manager Miller Huggins. It was, indeed, mirrored in the Yankees themselves that season as they wound up a dashing seventh in the American League.

It was either that spring or a year or so later that a rumor swept the Yankee bench that Ruth had died. These rumors, springing from no one knows where and traveling on the wings of the wind, are inevitable whenever a celebrity falls ill, even if it is with only a head cold. And Ruth was a celebrity and he had more than a head cold.

A rookie on the Yankee bench listened to the speculation which flew back and forth. In an effort to be facetious, or maybe, to pose as a callous, cynical man-of-the-world, he remarked to no one in particular:

"The big fellow dead? I suppose we'll have to chip in for flowers."

It probably was the last brash remark the young poseur ever uttered, for Waite Hoyt turned on him like a lion.

"Listen, punk," growled Hoyt, who could really turn it on when he wanted to, "Ruth has meant more to ball players than any man who ever lived. You ought to get down on your knees and thank God that a man like Babe existed. Where do you think you'd be if it hadn't been for the big fellow? Or where would I be? Or any of us? Or where would baseball be if it hadn't been for Babe?"

There was a heavy silence on the Yankee bench when Waite finished his outburst. It was particularly heavy in that corner of the bench where the pop-off kid was sitting.

Although the tummy ache heard around the world was the most famous of all Ruthian collapses, the Babe had a way of making all his ailments and injuries seem titanic. Everything Ruth did was dramatic. He probably was the only ball player since Abner Doubleday's time who could make a charley horse seem like a Greek tragedy.

On an April day in 1931 the Yankees were playing the Red Sox at Fenway Park. The sun was shining but it was raw and chilly in Boston, as it always seems to be up there to the outlander until about mid-August. The Babe was on third with one out and he took it into his head to score on a fly ball. It was a short fly. and Charley Berry, the Red Sox catcher, thought Babe was only going through the customary bluff when he made his run from third.

Berry, later to become an American League umpire of distinction, had been an All-America end at Lafayette College. Nature had built him not only well but solidly. He braced himself for the collision when it became evident that Ruth was going through with his bluff. The two met and there was a terrific crash. Charley, after first putting the ball on Babe, went flying in one direction, Ruth in another. An ambulance carted Ruth to the Peter Bent Brigham Hospital.

As was always the case when Ruth went down, you feared the worst. Babe was getting along in years now, as ball players go. He was in his late 30's and any injury might be his last as far as his baseball efficiency was concerned. He came out of this dramatic pile-up with an All-America football player with nothing worse than a badly bruised thigh and, when Berry and I went to visit him at the hospital next morning, he was sitting up in bed, joking with Mrs. Ruth and the nurse. His injured leg was encased in some electro-therapeutic device which looked like an illuminated doghouse.

The Babe was back in the game within a week, yet, as with almost any story dealing with Ruth, there was a story within a story. His injury touched off a chain of events which changed the entire careers of two ball players at least.

Ruth was injured on a Thursday and his place the next day in left field was taken by Myril Hoag, a young outfielder from the Pacific Coast League who had the smallest feet and one of the greatest throwing arms in the history of baseball. The Yanks won next day and Hoag made the final putout against the Red Sox, a gloved-hand stab of a line drive down the left field foul line.

Hoag twisted his ankle making this catch but, since it was the last out of the game, nobody in the press box realized it until the next day

Keystone

After colliding with Catcher Berry at Fenway Park, April 22, 1931, Ruth attempted to take his outfield position and then collapsed. He is being carted from the field to an ambulance by Trainer Painter and teammates.

when Myril was unable to play. Joe McCarthy, in his first year of managing the Yankees, now had lost two outfielders in two days.

On Saturday, the Yankees were beaten in extra innings in the last game of the Boston series when Ben Chapman, playing second base, first fumbled a ground ball and then pulled a skull by throwing the batter out at first base while allowing the winning Red Sox run to come home from third to end the game.

From Boston the Yankees went to Washington for a Sunday game. It was a rainy, murky day but Clark Griffith had most of his tickets sold in advance (on the strength of Ruth making his first appearance of the year there) and he was going to play, come high-water or more high-water. Those rain checks were not going to be redeemable.

The game got under way about an hour late. In one of the early innings, Dusty Cooke, a promising outfielder, attempted to make a diving catch of a fly hit by a Washington player and crashed to the wet and slippery turf with a broken collarbone. Thus did McCarthy lose his third outfielder in four days.

In desperation, McCarthy sent Chapman to the outfield to take Cooke's place. Chapman had come to the Yankees from St. Paul the year before as an infielder with a reputation for power and great speed, both of which he showed in quantity during the 1930 season under Bob Shawkey. McCarthy, however, had been an infielder himself and he was never quite sold on Ben as an infielder. Chapman's play against the Red Sox the day before had about convinced Joe that Ben's power and speed would have to be capitalized on in some other position.

From the very first, Chapman clicked as an outfielder. He stole sixty-one bases for the Yankees in that 1931 season, batted .315 and hit seventeen home runs. He never again went back to the infield but remained an outfielder to the end of his major league days. When Ben was through as a big leaguer, he came back after a spell in the minors as a pitcher and wound up as manager of the Phillies.

Cooke who, like Chapman, had speed and power, never recovered from that injury in Washington, Dusty and Ben were buddies and one of Chapman's first acts as a major league manager was to have Dusty added to the Phillies' staff as a trainer. Cooke took his duties as a Philadelphia trainer seriously enough to get himself thrown out of a game in Brooklyn in the 1946 season.

It is somewhat ironic that Ruth's injury in Boston should have touched off the chain of events which made Chapman, the misfit infielder, an outfield star and the leading base stealer of his time in the majors, for Ben and the Babe never hit it off. It was Chapman who, a couple of years later, attempted to get up a petition among the other Yankee players asking Ruth to bench himself for the good of the team!

The legend of Ruth as the stricken warrior is another of the many myths surrounding the great man. Barring the season of 1925, the year of the big tummy ache, and 1922 when Commissioner Landis grounded him for forty days and forty nights, the Babe played as many ball games per season as the average American League regular. Though he was indisposed for a day here and a couple of days there, only once in his fifteen seasons with the Yankees was he on the bench when he might have helped the club. And that, strangely enough, was in 1921 when Ruth had batted the Bombers to the first of their many American League championships.

Ruth entered the World Series against the Giants that season in bad shape. He had a boil on his left elbow and a wrenched knee, either injury painful enough to cause a lesser ball player to sit out the Series. But Ruth was Ruth and he went through the first five games of the Series, quitting only when it was obvious that he couldn't help the ball club. While Babe was in there, he was a big lift to the Yanks, leading the club in hitting, batting one homer and stealing two bases. When Babe bowed out, the Yanks had a three to two edge over the Giants but the National Leaguers took the next three games to win

Press Association

Ruth never got the credit he deserved for his superb judgment on the bases. He is shown here stealing home against the Browns in 1932, by which time he was nearing forty. Rick Ferrell is the catcher and Frankie Crosetti the hitter.

the Series by five games to three. It is reasonable enough to suppose that Ruth, had he been able to play in all the games, might have meant the difference which would have given the championship to the Yankees.

While Ruth was in there in this Series, he singled home a first-inning run to get the Yanks off in front against Phil Douglas in the opener, a game which the underhander, Carl Mays, won by 3 to 0. Walked three times in the second game, which the Yanks won by the same score as the opener, the Babe took advantage of his time on the base paths to demonstrate once and for all, if any doubters remained, that he was a ball player, rather than just a big clown who had an extraordinary gift for hitting home runs. In this game Babe stole second and third in succession in one inning. Another time he did a splendid piece of base running to go from first to third on an ordinary single by Bob Meusel. The Giants had to make a play on Babe at third and the throw-in enabled Meusel to take second and served to set up a two-run inning for the Yanks.

It was a remarkable demonstration for a ball player with a wrenched knee and an infected elbow. Perhaps the best proof of Ruth's value was the fact that the Yanks couldn't win another game in the Series after he took to the sidelines.

If Ruth had a hangnail, writers covering the Yankees rushed to the wires with at least a one-column box on the agonies and travails of the great man. If he was observed taking an aspirin it was practically a scoop for the writer who saw him reach for the sedative. Now the writers covering the Yanks weren't acting like Boy Scouts at these manifestations of human frailty on the part of the Bambino. Everybody in America was interested in the well-being of Babe Ruth, particularly those gentlemen who owned ball parks in which he was to appear in the near future. Ruth was news, national news, as no ball player ever has been, before or since.

The natural consequence this minute reporting on the state of Babe's health was to give not only the casual fan but the addict as well the impression that Ruth was forever on the point of taking to his bed, there to pluck languidly at the counterpane and pine away.

Actually, such was far from the case. Without recourse to ponderous research, it is safe to say that between 1919 when Ed Barrow first planted Babe permanently in the outfield and 1935 when he left the

Yankees, Ruth played more games than any contemporary American Leaguer. He rarely played less than 140 games a season and six times played over 150. And this out of a schedule of 154 games.

Lou Gehrig, famed in song and story, and in celluloid, as the Iron Horse, compiled the most amazing record for durability of anyone in the history of baseball. He played 2130 championship games in succession, a record which, like Ruth's 714 home runs, will exist until they change the basic pattern of baseball. Lou became a regular five years after Babe joined the Yankees and continued as a regular five years after his home run partner had left the team. As a Yankee, Gehrig played 2164 games, while Ruth appeared in 2084 games as a Yank.

This comparison isn't meant to set up Ruth as a rival in endurance to Lou, since there is no comparison along those lines between Gehrig and Ruth or between Gehrig and anybody. It is brought out only to show that Babe didn't spend all of his time as a Yankee in sick bay. It only seemed that way to one who was constantly reading clinical items about the big fellow on the sports pages.

Babe started to slip when Joe McCarthy came to the Yankees but it wasn't all cause and effect. The years were catching up with Ruth by then. He was thirty-six and the bay window was becoming more and more difficult for his pipestem legs to lug around. He managed to give McCarthy 145 games in Joe's first year with the club, 1931, the year of Babe's crack-up with Berry in Boston. He never played as many as 140 games again and by 1934, he was in only 125 games and fell below .300 for the second time since he had left the pitcher's mound to become an outfielder. In this last season as a Yankee, Babe hit only *(sic)* 22 home runs, a total which was good enough to give another Yankee, Nick Etten, the home run championship of the American League a cool ten years later in the war-torn season of 1944.

One plate at which Babe never slumped was the one on the dining room table. As long as the big fellow stayed in the big leagues, he ate like a big leaguer. Anybody who ever was privileged to see Ruth with a knife and fork knew they were looking at a champion. He ate catch-as-catch can, with no holds barred, and was as impressive disposing of food as he was knocking baseballs out of sight.

The legend of the eighteen frankfurters seemed perfectly plausible to anybody who had been treated to an exhibition of Ruth's Gargantuan appetite. Down at Dover Hall, the hunting plantation near

Keystone

As a nimrod, and trencherman at the table, Ruth made a great reputation for himself at Uncle Robbie's Dover Hall hunting lodge. Left to right: Colonel Charley Crowley, William J. (Bunk) Macbeth and the Babe.

Brunswick, Ga., where Uncle Wilbert Robinson, Falstaffian manager of the Dodgers, was wont to make his winter home, old survivors still talk in awed tones of Ruth's eating prowess. And this was achieved in an eating league where they played hard ball, for Uncle Robbie himself was a prodigious trencherman and none of his cronies, Col. Til Huston, Ban Johnson, Bozeman Bulger or Irvin S. Cobb, ever pulled away from the plate.

Ruth, however, never claimed any eating titles. In fact, the Babe never saw anything unusual in the amount of calories he needed to stoke the engine that constituted his amazing body. He had an appreciation of a good "doer" at the table as the following story shows.

In the spring of 1934, the Yankees played an exhibition game against the Chattanooga Lookouts in the Tennessee ball park presided over by Joe Engel, the man who had first seen Ruth pitch when Big George was the sensation of St. Mary's Industrial Home. One of the visitors to the game was a short, roundish man who shyly came up to greet the Babe. He was Sammy Vick, whose place Ruth had taken in the Yankee lineup when he was sold by the Red Sox to New York. This is entirely irrelevant to the story but the name of Sammy Vick was as well known to night sports editors on the desks of metropolitan newspapers as that of Ruth because of the midnight habit of beer-drinking fans telephoning to settle the bet as to the name of the Yankee right fielder whose place had been taken by Ruth.

Vick extended his hand and received a hearty shake from Ruth in return.

"Hi ya, keed!" said the Babe.

"Don't give me that 'Hi ya, keed' stuff," said Sammy. "Why, you big baboon, you don't even know who I am."

"The hell I don't," retorted Ruth. "I may have forgotten your name but I know who you are, all right. You're the guy who could eat more than any other two so-and-sos I ever saw!"

His identity thus established, Vick and the Babe had quite a chat.

Ruth came out of quasi-retirement in mid-season of 1938 to serve as coach of the Brooklyn Dodgers, and he quickly made it known that his years away from baseball hadn't served to take the edge off his appetite.

One of Ruth's duties with the Dodgers was to play first base in the night exhibition games booked by Larry MacPhail, so that there might be a substantial return on the $15,000 Babe received for the last three and a half months of the season.

Ruth earned his bread and butter one night in Syracuse but decided to make it steak and potatoes instead. He invited John McDonald, the Dodger road secretary, to be his guest for a midnight snack after the game. John, whose many services to MacPhail stopped just short of requiring him to be in uniform for night exhibition games, told Babe that he would eat his dinner before the game but would meet Babe in his room afterward anyway.

"It's a good thing I had eaten beforehand," related McDonald afterward. "At first I thought the Babe had misunderstood me because when the waiter brought the food up, he came with doubles—double shrimp cocktail, double order of hash-browned potatoes, double order of spinach and a planked steak for two. When I saw Ruth sit down, however, I realized he had known I'd already eaten and had made no provisions for me.

"Ruth finished everything so thoroughly the waiter could have put the dishes right back on the shelf. Pie à la mode and a full pot of coffee completed the meal. Babe then took out a huge Corona, lit it and began to discuss the ball club with me.

"He paused in the middle of a sentence, excused himself and went to the medicine cabinet in the bathroom. He returned with a bottle of some white, gooey stuff, holding it out to me so I could read the label.

"I saw that it was some sort of prescription, prepared by Babe's physician for him and that the directions read, 'One teaspoonful in water after meals.'

"Babe told me it was some sort of an aid to digestion. And then, without further ado, he put the bottle to his lips, tilted his head, and polished off the entire contents. He then tossed the empty into the wastebasket, winked at me and said, 'Tomorrow, kid, the fur'll fly!' "

7

The Big Hello

At the conclusion of World War I, Ferdinand Foch held the title of Marshal of France and Generalissimo of the Allied and Associated Powers on the Western Front. He probably was as well known to the American people as our own General Pershing. When he visited the United States in 1921 he was wildly acclaimed in one city after another. It was inevitable that on his New York visit he should be taken to the Polo Grounds to meet Babe Ruth, then in his second year with the Yankees and in the process of bringing them their first American League pennant by the simple process of belting the ears off any pitcher rash enough to throw the ball within a bat's length of the plate. Everybody who came to New York in those days visited the Polo Grounds to see Ruth, just as they made it a point to see the Aquarium and the Bronx Zoo. Of the three, Ruth was the most interesting.

It was a stirring, if somewhat inarticulate, moment when the Marshal of France and the King of Swat clasped hands for the benefit of posterity, with cameras ready to record an entirely new phase of Franco-American relations. The Marshal knew a few words of English, none of which seemed to pertain to baseball. The Babe knew no French and precious few words of English which did not pertain to baseball. It looked like a conversational impasse.

Ruth rose to the occasion. Grasping the hand of Marshal Foch firmly, doffing his cap politely and serving his most charming grin, the Babe asked, "You were in the war, weren't you?"

"Oui, oui," replied the Marshal and what might have been an international crisis was averted.

Ruth's inability to recall names was legendary. He would never have remembered Addison Sims of Seattle, the fellow who used to pop up in all those ads for mail-order memory courses years ago. He probably wouldn't even have remembered Seattle. It wasn't entirely a faulty memory as much as it was mental carelessness. The Babe never made any effort to memorize the names of people, probably because he figured that the next time he saw them they'd remember him and there was no sense in the two of them worrying about such trivial details.

Proof that Babe's inability to recall names wasn't entirely due to a faulty memory was his greeting to Sammy Vick in Chattanooga, mentioned in the previous chapter. Ruth had taken Vick's place in the Yankee outfield, had played against him in the American League and had every reason to remember his name. Babe, of course, didn't remember his name, but he did remember Sammy's appetite. Obviously, therefore, he knew who Vick was.

It wasn't merely ball players or writers or fans whose names Ruth forgot, or neglected to recall, if you prefer. He once told Herb Pennock he was having dinner with "those movie people." Pennock, knowing Babe well, was more than mildly interested. Herb knew that "those movie people," in the big fellow's vague and sweeping generality, could be actors, actresses, directors, producers or maybe somebody no more important than the ticket-taker and usher at a neighborhood house. So the quiet Pennock did a little investigating on his own. "Those movie people" turned out to be Douglas Fairbanks and Mary Pickford, then at the very zenith of their popularity.

There was no offense meant, nor did Ruth intend any brush-off. And it wasn't that he was letting a sense of his own importance run away with him, either. He was just no hand with names. There was an occasion when a Governor of some Southern state visited the Yankee bench and Babe escorted him along the line, introducing him to the other members of the club.

Ruth was getting along famously with his gubernatorial chum until

Keystone

One name the Babe never forgot was that of Eddie Bennett, the little hunchback who was mascot for the pennant winning Yanks of Miller Huggins' era.

he ran across Mike Gazella, the old Lafayette football star who then was in his third or fourth season as a utility infielder with the Yanks.

"And this, Governor," said the Babe, "is, er—is—say, keed, what the hell's your name again?"

At some point in his career Ruth developed a technique to cover the myriad situations in which he didn't know the name of the person who greeted him. He gave everybody the "Hi ya, keed!" That became the big fellow's blanket greeting. It worked rather well, too. Those who had been familiar with Ruth for a number of years learned to accept it as standard and those who were renewing an acquaintance with Ruth which had been of rather brief duration merely thought that Babe was rather breezily informal.

During the 1930 World Series between the Athletics and the Cardinals, Ruth was seated in the press box, "ghosting" the Series for the Christy Walsh Syndicate. Moe Berg, then catching for the White Sox, happened to run across Babe as he was trying to find his own location.

"Hello, Babe," grinned Moe.

"Hi ya, keed," replied the literary lion.

Berg laughed outright and Ruth turned quickly to face him again.

"Oh, it's you," said Babe, seizing Berg's arm and then pausing as he tried to recall the name of the catcher. Suddenly a grin broke out on his big moon face and he burst into a little jingle. "Moe, Moe, he gets the dough!" Ruth was as proud of that spot identification as if he had invented the Bertillon system.

Nobody ever was offended when Babe forgot his name. He once stumbled over the name of a fellow with whom he had been playing golf for three straight autumns, missing his name as completely as though the chap had suddenly appeared out of thin air.

The most famous of all Ruth's misadventures with names, of course, was his famous errand of mercy to Johnny Sylvester, a boy who lay dying in a New Jersey town not far from New York. The boy had been operated upon and had lost the will to live. Like any other ten-year-old boy in America, Babe Ruth was his idol. Somebody—the doctor, a relative, his father—had the thought that perhaps a personal visit from his hero would restore in the child the will to live.

Word was brought to Ruth at Yankee Stadium and early next morning Babe was at the boy's bedside. Paul Gallico, a sports writer who was to go on to bigger and greater things, grew positively lyrical describing the visit in his column in the New York *Daily News.* Wrote Paul:

> . . . It was God himself who walked into the room, straight from His glittering throne, God dressed in a camel's hair polo coat and flat camel's hair cap, God with a big flat nose and little piggy eyes and a big grin, with a fat, black cigar sticking out of the side of it.

The Babe sat down alongside the boy whose life had been despaired of and talked to him. He answered questions and gave him, of all things, a baseball bat, telling him he expected the boy would soon be well enough to use it. He autographed a baseball. He told young Johnny about the Yankees and he gave him some advice, advice that he himself never bothered about, advice such as listening to the doctor, obeying his elders and taking care of himself. And he promised young Johnny Sylvester that he would hit a home run for him that very afternoon at Yankee Stadium.

Promising to hit a home run was routine stuff with Ruth those days because he was hitting home runs almost every afternoon, whether on promise or not. And if he didn't hit one on that particular afternoon, he was almost a cinch to hit one tomorrow or certainly by the day after tomorrow.

Ruth, as a matter of fact, did hit a home run for Johnny Sylvester that very afternoon. And Johnny, brightening visibly after the visit from Ruth, shook off his post-operation lassitude and started on the long road back to recovery.

The newspapers got hold of the story and played it up with the expected symphonic accompaniment of slow music and tugs at the heart strings. There were some who saw in the entire episode a gigantic publicity plot, which simply was not so at all. There was a Johnny Sylvester, he was dying and he did recover. And Babe did hit a homer the afternoon of the same day on which he visited him. Ruth told nobody about the visit, or at least didn't mention the visit with the intention of receiving any extra-curricular publicity, for the Babe didn't need any, then or ever. There were times, of course, when the big fellow was bamboozled into being a stooge for various publicity stunts but never for himself.

There are two sequels to Ruth's 1926 errand of mercy to the dying Johnny Sylvester. The first happened the following spring, the second two decades later. On the first visit of the Yankees to Philadelphia in 1927, Babe was approached by a well-dressed, middle-aged gentleman who introduced himself as Johnny Sylvester's uncle.

"I thought you'd like to know, Mr. Ruth," said the gentleman, "that Johnny is making a remarkable recovery. He certainly would want me to thank you and I want to thank you on behalf of the family."

"That's fine," replied the Babe. "I'm certainly glad to hear it. You tell Johnny I was asking for him and telling him to keep up the good work."

They shook hands and parted. Babe gazed after the retreating figure of the courteous gentleman, scratched his head and murmured puzzledly, "Now who the hell is Johnny Sylvester?"

This isn't to be taken as an indication that Babe had forgotten all about his visit to the sick and dying boy the previous year. Had somebody explained to Ruth that Johnny was the boy he had gone over to Jersey to see, the chances are Ruth would have instantly recalled the incident. It was merely the name he couldn't place.

When Ruth began his eighty-two-day stay in New York's French Hospital in late November of 1946, few outside of his own family realized that the home run king was gravely ill. The early announcements from the hospital were routine and it was assumed Babe's stay there would be a matter of days. Rae O. Weimer, managing editor of *The Newspaper PM,* thought he had dug up a tip-top human interest story by discovering the whereabouts of the long-since-forgotten Johnny Sylvester, who was now living and working in Queens in New York City.

Weimer thought it would be a good story to have Sylvester visit the big fellow, a sort of bread-cast-upon-the-waters angle in which the boy, now grown to manhood, returned the visit that Ruth had made to him twenty years before. It was only after talking to Ruth's family that we discovered the "No Visitors" edict was not merely a device to keep out the curious. The Babe was in tough shape.

Sylvester, incidentally, wanted to visit the Babe on his own, without publicity. Johnny, now thirty years old, wished no photographers or write-ups, but merely to tell the sick man that it had been his visit twenty years before which had fired a dying boy with the will to live. He was genuinely distressed when he learned of the gravity of Ruth's condition. Eventually, under the auspices of the *Daily News,* Johnny did get to visit Babe after the big fellow had left the hospital.

To really know what sort of man Ruth was, you have to understand that his affection for children was sincere. The Babe, for all of

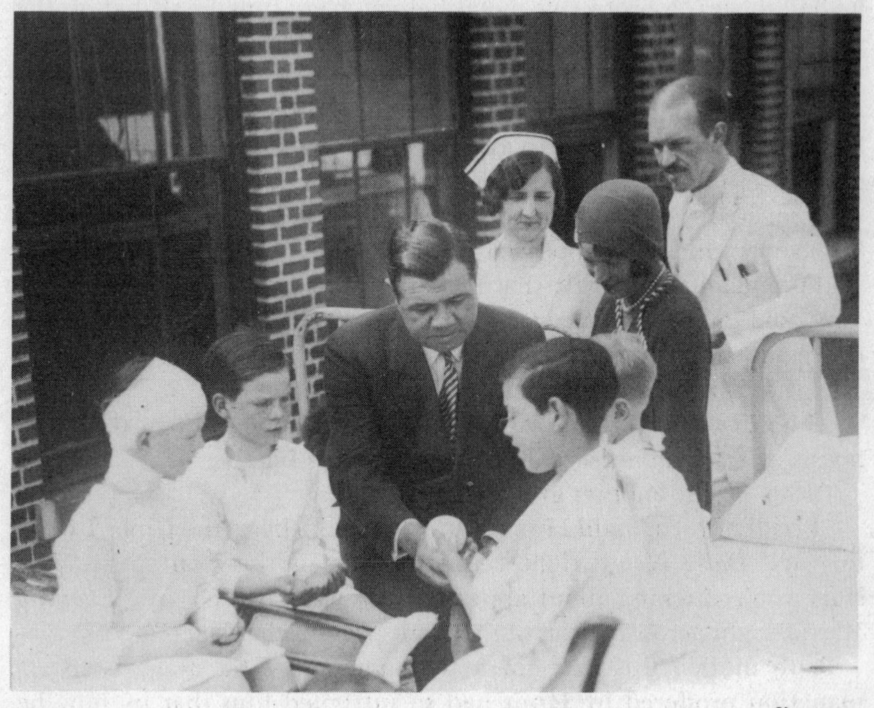

Keystone

Babe and Clair visiting youngsters at New York's Knickerbocker Hospital. The big fellow was always available when the kids wanted him.

his lusty living, for all of his bluff and often crude ways, had ever a soft spot in his heart for kids. Every public appearance Ruth made, in his playing days or thereafter, was an inconvenience and an annoyance but Babe never once turned down a promise to go somewhere and visit the kids, unless it was because he had a previous obligation to visit kids somewhere else.

It is fashionable to be cynical and there are many who would sooner retell the story of Ruth forgetting the name of Johnny Sylvester than tell the story of his original visit, a visit which saved the life of a boy who had just come through a serious head operation, a boy who was to grow up to an athletic career of his own despite that handicap, who was to become a better than average hockey player, even though he had to wear a protective metal helmet every time he skated on the rink.

The Babe knew the names of most of the newspapermen who traveled with the Yankees regularly, knew their nicknames, too, although he often found it difficult to associate them with the papers by which they were employed. I recall one time when he called Marshall Hunt, who covered the Yankees for the morning tabloid, the *Daily News,* for a story which had appeared in the old New York *Evening World.* Hunt explained patiently that he hadn't written the article.

"Look, Babe," Hunt said, "I work for the *Daily News.* It comes out in the mornings. It's a tabloid—about so big."

"Yeah," grunted the Babe.

"The *Evening World,"* continued Hunt, "comes out in the afternoons. It's a standard-sized paper—about this big."

"Yeah," came another grunt.

"Besides which," said Hunt, as the final clincher, "the paper I work for says *'Daily News'* right across the top of the front page. The story you're kicking about appeared in a paper which says *'Evening World'* right across the top of the front page. Is that clear?"

Ruth mulled this over for a few moments. The step-by-step explanation proffered by Hunt had so intrigued him that by now he probably had forgotten his original objections to the story in the *Evening World.*

"Even so," answered Babe, "you fellows shouldn't write anything unless you know all the facts."

And with that journalistic pontification, Ruth allowed the matter to drop. It was, by the way, good advice to all writers, sports or otherwise, then or now.

There was, writing baseball on the New York *Post* in the mid-30's, a young man named Charles (Mike) Houston who came from Norfolk and left New York to work in Richmond, after covering himself with glory by being the only sports writer in America to pick the New York

Giants and the Washington Senators as the 1933 pennant winners. There was, and still is, around New York a baseball writer named Ken Smith of the *Daily Mirror*. The only resemblance between the two was that both were short, with Smitty being appreciably the shorter of the two. Both had dark hair but Mike had much more of it and a mustache to boot.

One day in the summer of 1934, while the Yankees were playing a series in Washington, Houston drove up from Richmond with his wife and sister-in-law to visit with his cronies in the press box. After the ball game, back at the Shoreham Hotel, Mike announced that he was going to see Babe Ruth for a minute or two, because his sister-in-law had never met the great man.

Houston's visit with Ruth lasted over an hour and Mike came back to the lobby practically gurgling with glee over the hospitable reception Babe and Mrs. Ruth had extended to his family.

"You know," confided Mike, "it's over a year since I had seen the big fellow and I was afraid that he wouldn't remember me, which would have been an awful let-down for me in front of my sister-in-law. He couldn't have been nicer to us."

On the Yankee bench the following afternoon, Ruth turned to one of the writers and said, "You'll never guess who came up to visit me last night—Smitty!"

There is no telling how far Houston might have been let down had he known that Ruth was entertaining him, the sports columnist of the Richmond *Times-Dispatch,* under the impression that he was Ken Smith, who was covering the Giants some 200-odd miles away!

While on the subject of Ruth and names it may be interesting to know how the Yankees themselves addressed royalty. Babe, to most of his teammates, was known as "Jidge" and sometimes "Jidgie." There never has been any satisfactory explanation for this nickname, although Ruth always accepted it. My impression was that it might have been a corruption of Judge, a nickname in sports which is usually hung on outsized athletes. However, Fred Lieb, a baseball historian who knew Ruth back in the days when he was breaking in with the Red Sox, believes the tag was given to Ruth by George Mogridge, the left-handed pitcher, who was one of Babe's teammates when he first came to the Yankees in 1920.

"Jidge" was rarely used when talking about Ruth, only when talk-

Culver Service

Mound staff of the 1915 World Champion Red Sox. Left to right: George Foster, Carl Mays, Ernie Shore, Babe's first roommate, the Babe, and Hubert (Dutch) Leonard, his second roommate.

ing to him. In conversation among players he usually was referred to as "Babe" or "the Babe" but even more frequently as "the big fellow." If you mentioned "the big fellow" to anybody in the American League over the twenty-year period when Ruth was hitting home runs, he'd have known instantly whom you meant.

That Ruth accepted this inexplicable nickname of "Jidge" is indicated by the present he made of a Mexican hairless dog to Lou Gehrig's mother. He informed Ma Gehrig that the dog's name was "Jidge," although what resemblance there could possibly be between a tiny Chihuahua and the big hulk of man that was Ruth is more than a little mystifying.

There is an old baseball story, probably even pre-Ring Lardner, about Ossie Schreckengrost, a catcher who conferred a boon upon linotypists by changing his name to Schreck, refusing to room with

Rube Waddell, the great but peculiar southpaw, unless it were specified in the latter's contract that he refrain from eating animal crackers in bed.

It never has been established that Ruth ever ate animal crackers in bed but he had several other habits which made him, if not undesirable, at least a trying roommate. His first roommate in the major leagues was Ernie Shore, the pitcher who had come up from Baltimore to the Red Sox with the Babe, and who later was to return to his native Winston-Salem, leaving a fine pitching record behind and carrying some amazing memories with him. Shore is now a sheriff in Winston-Salem but it is doubtful if his experiences in enforcing law and order in that North Carolina municipality have been half as trying as those he underwent when trying to get a good night's sleep with the Babe as a roommate.

Shore finally told Manager Carrigan he was leaving the club. Rough was startled and inquired as to the cause.

"It's that Ruth," explained Ernie, "I can't live with that man."

Carrigan was astounded and, seeking further details, found that Ruth never bothered to distinguish between toothbrushes in the bathroom rack, using the one which was nearest, much to the distress of the outraged Carolinian. The Babe was then teamed up with Dutch Leonard, a left-hander, who either was made of sterner stuff than Shore or else hid his toothbrush under the pillow nights.

It may be as well to bring up here and now the fact that this same Shore, through the youthful impetuosity of Ruth, has his name in the record books as the author of a unique no-hitter, a perfect game in which Ernie faced only twenty-six batsmen but received credit for retiring twenty-seven!

Ruth was scheduled to pitch the first game of a double header against Washington on a Saturday afternoon, June 23, 1917. Eddie Foster was the first batter for the visiting Senators and therefore the first batter of the ball game.

Foster worked Ruth for a base on balls and Babe didn't like the call Umpire Owens gave the fourth ball. Owens, who was christened Clarence but insisted on being called Brick for obvious reasons, found himself confronted by a very indignant young giant of twenty-two.

Ruth told Owens what he thought of him personally and of his immediate ancestors, if any. Owens, whose childhood back of the Yards in Chicago, hadn't been entirely wasted, retorted in kind. The next thing Brick knew Ruth had thrown a punch at him. Since Ban Johnson, president of the American League, had put the sanctity of the umpires even before the sanctity of the home, Ruth was out of the game in no time, eventually to be suspended for a week and fined $100, a comparatively mild penalty for his offense.

Jack Barry, the baseball genius who was later to produce so many stars at Holy Cross, was managing Boston and he hurriedly warmed up Shore to replace the banished Ruth. Foster, who had drawn the controversial base on balls, was caught stealing and not another Washingtonian reached first base. There was much wrangling as to whether Shore should be credited with a perfect game or not, inasmuch as only 26 men faced him, but he finally received credit for it. In the three decades of major league baseball since then, there has been only one other perfect game.

If Ruth was difficult to room with, he was exciting as a traveling companion. Babe made it a regular habit to demolish every straw hat he found in the clubhouse or on the Pullmans after Labor Day. It was in the process of carrying out this demolition celebration one September that Mike McNally, a teammate of Babe's both with the Red Sox and the Yankees, attempted to teach Babe a lesson. It didn't cure Ruth of his love for destruction, but it did cure him of ever wearing a straw hat again.

The Yankees were coming back from Boston on a sleeper this particular September in the early 20's when Ruth, first craftily hiding his own dicer in an upper berth, decided it was time to declare a closed season, or an open one, on straw hats and went from car to car smashing every player's straw hat he could lay his hands on.

McNally had observed where the big fellow had cached his own straw hat. When Ruth had retired, Mike retrieved the hat and took it to the dining car where he wrangled from a sleepy chef a quantity of eggs, some catsup and any other condiments that he was able to scrape up. The entire mess—and mess is a far more apt term than melange—was poured into Babe's hat and thoroughly scrambled. Then the hat was restored to its original hiding place.

The next morning Ruth arose, dressed himself and, reaching jauntily into the upper, grabbed his hat.

"There's no flies on the old Babe," said Ruth, clamping the loaded hat upon his head. There weren't any flies on Babe but there was practically everything else, as the mess trickled slowly down through his hair, over his eyes and into his ears.

Since nothing ordinary ever happened to Ruth it developed that he had to appear in court that morning as a witness against an Italian truck driver whose vehicle had crashed into Ruth's car while it was parked. There was no chance to change his clothes, nor any time for thorough ablutions. Babe just washed the mess out of his hair and from his face and clothes as best he could.

It was a warm morning in the traffic court, unseasonably so, and for once the big Bam was not the center of attraction. Gradually those next to the great man moved away. Babe beckoned a court attendant and asked him if the case could be dismissed.

"But you aren't suing him, Mr. Ruth," explained the court attendant. "You're only here as a witness. The man was driving without a license."

"Look, keed," wheedled the Babe in his best legal manner, "I don't care what the charge is. Tell the Judge I'll pay that guy's fine, only please let me get out of here and get this suit changed."

Another celebration conceived by Ruth was that of ripping to shreds the shirts of his teammates after they had won a pennant. It came to pass that the Yankees won pennants so frequently that the Babe felt constrained to change the rules. Thereafter, he ripped the shirts from the backs of his teammates only after they had won a World Series. It was an impressive sight to see the big fellow galumphing through a train, going from car to car and denuding his fellow Yankees of their shirts at one fell swoop. As each player and his shirt parted company, he promptly fell in with the Babe's impromptu snake dance, lending willing and enthusiastic hands as the next shirt was to be separated from its owner.

Ruth was no respecter of persons in these shirt-snatching tours, either. Colonel Ruppert locked himself in his stateroom returning from one World Series, lest he fall a victim to the Babe's ebullience.

Curiously enough, this ritual ceased when Ruth left the Yankees. His last tour of vandalism was in 1932, on the way home from Chicago after the Yanks had cleaned up the Cubs four straight. In their next three World Series, 1936, 1937 and 1938, the Yankees had no opportunity for such horseplay with the haberdashery because they won the deciding game of each of those Series in New York.

A half-hearted attempt was made to revive this traditional victory ritual of the Yankees on the way back to New York from Cincinnati after they had won the World Series in four straight in 1939. The celebrants had just about started their march when Joe McCarthy broke it up. Joe had been sitting by himself, brooding perhaps over the fact that this undoubtedly was the last trip Lou Gehrig ever would make as a Yankee.

The noise and general whoop-tee-doo the celebrants made penetrated into McCarthy's drawing room. He opened the door, stuck out his head, surveyed the merry-makers and remarked caustically:

"I thought I was managing a major league ball club."

P.S.: There was no shirt-snatching parade.

Keystone

Under the influence of his second wife, Clair, Ruth became a homebody. Here he is, in smoking jacket, cutting a cake on his thirty-ninth birthday.

Because Babe Ruth was a big overgrown kid, full of animal spirits and cursed with an inability to remember names, don't ever get the idea that he was a dope. Far from it. Ruth's I.Q. would have stood up with that of the average ball player had there been anyone brash enough to submit the big fellow to a Binet test.

Ruth's instinctive flair for baseball, which will be dealt with at length in a later chapter, is common knowledge. Few, however, knew that Babe had an excellent understanding of football, although he never played the game. And, although it was vine leaves, rather than ivy, which one would expect to find sprouting from the Babe's locks, he attended something like fifteen successive Harvard-Yale football games. Despite the fact that he turned up annually at Cambridge or the Bowl in New Haven, he never gave any inkling as to whether his sympathies lay with Fair Harvard or the Bulldog of Yale. And when the Army-Notre Dame game was played at Yankee Stadium, the Babe was right there with the rest of the subway alumni.

Until the time he entered French Hospital in 1946 Ruth was a diligent bowler. He began playing the pin game back in 1915 when he first joined the Red Sox and although his interest waned later in favor of other nocturnal recreations he eventually came back to his first love.

Next to baseball, Babe was prouder of his golfing achievements than of any other athletic skill. He could hit a ball a mile off the tee and was fairly sharp on the greens, although his short game was not steady. Ruth frequently shot in the low 70's but the very inconsistencies which made him such a spectacular performer in baseball hampered his progress in golf, where the rule is that *all* the strokes must be counted. In baseball, Babe could take two strikes and then hit the ball out of the park, or pop up three times and then come through with a game-winning homer.

Ruth was an almost daily golfer from the time he quit baseball (or vice versa) until his doctors ordered him to take it easy. Even after his ravaging illness, when Babe flew to Miami Beach to convalesce, he played nine holes in 45, a score any duffer would be proud of and a truly remarkable round for a man who had lingered in a hospital for eighty-two days and had been home from the hospital less than two months.

Charley Segar, who traveled with the Yankees for years as correspondent for the *Daily Mirror,* and who now heads the National League press bureau, tells of a shot Ruth made at the Jungle Club in St. Pete, playing in a foursome with Segar, Fred Lieb and Jeff Mosher, sports editor of the St. Petersburg *Independent.* The Babe shot a two on a par five hole and, in typical Ruthian fashion, did it the hard way, too. His drive from the tee was some 275 yards, but behind some traps. Taking a No. 2, Ruth shot for the green, still 215 yards distant, and not only made it but put the ball in the cup as well.

There are countless stories of Ruth's fist fights but the bald truth is that he had remarkably few, certainly no more, per season, than the average ball player. Ball players, contrary to popular belief, are not too handy with their dukes. The most widely publicized fist fight between ball players took place many years ago between Ty Cobb and Buck Herzog when the Tigers and Giants came north together. The two belligerents were locked in a hotel room, with a third ball player, mutually agreeable to both contestants, to see that neither killed the other. When time was called, each was more exhausted than battered and the general opinion of those who had heard all versions, including the referee's, was that it would have required a great deal less formidable an opponent than the famed gorilla of the late Arthur Brisbane to "lick them both."

About the best that can be said for Ruth as a fighter was said a long time ago about another very colorful ball player, the late John J. McGraw. It was Sid Mercer who once remarked of the Little Napoleon, "That he never ducked a fight and never won one."

The only record of Ruth ever ducking a fight was that day back in 1918 when Ed Barrow, then managing the Red Sox, cleared the clubhouse and took off his coat so that he might personally prove to the big fellow that it would be better for all hands if Ruth should show himself amenable to authority. Barrow won't talk about it but the consensus is that Ruth, realizing he was wrong, passed up the challenge.

Wally Pipp, a teammate and the Yankee whom Gehrig replaced at first base when he started his amazing string of consecutive games, once flattened the Babe. Pipp, a high-class ball player and a high-class gentleman, resented something Babe said but there was no feud between the two and the incident was passed off. Ruth never was one to hold a grudge and nobody could hold a grudge against the big guy.

There was a certain coolness between Tris Speaker and Ruth because Babe thought the Texan was riding him when he first came up from "The Home" and the two were never really friendly until almost twenty years after. In later days, on the Yanks, Babe and Ben Chapman didn't hit it off at all, but it never got beyond the wordy and sulky stage.

There was one night in St. Louis when the Yanks were leaving

Keystone

Christy Walsh, the man who taught Ruth that money could be saved as well as spent, pictured with the big fellow in Los Angeles. Christy often has been considered the greatest single influence on the Babe.

from the Delmar Station, back in 1931. Jimmy Reese, a young infielder from the Coast, had attached himself to the Babe, and Babe and Mrs. Ruth found the personable youngster excellent company. Jimmy had a real hero worshipper's slant toward Ruth and used to make certain that the multitudinous traveling impedimenta of the Ruths got from hotel to station safely.

Reese showed up at the Delmar Station that night with some grip or other that the Ruths had overlooked and somebody in the assembled crowd (I never could be sure but I always thought it was Chapman) made a crack to Reese about being Babe's caddy. There was a lot of spunk to Jimmy and he flared right back.

I happened to catch the Babe's face when this hot exchange took place. His beady eyes flamed and I thought surely he was going to declare himself. And then he sort of shrugged his shoulders, walked over to a golf bag, picked up his driver and proceeded to tee up a golf ball on the tracks. He leaned into the ball and hit it out of sight, no great trick since this was about ten o'clock at night, and the caddy conversation subsided as quickly as it had started. I've always thought that Babe had intended to take a hand that night but thought better of it.

Every once in a while, either with or without the blessing of his manager, Christy Walsh, Ruth was moved to public utterance in favor of a political candidate. For the record, the Babe hasn't had a winner yet and I don't think Walsh has had one either.

The first manifestation of any interest by Babe in the body politic came at the conclusion of the 1928 World Series, as the Yankees were speeding home from St. Louis, after another of their justly celebrated four-straight sweeps. There were high jinks on the train that night. The beer flowed freely and the shirts had been stripped from all hands. As the Yankee Special paused at Terre Haute a crowd of fans, numbering over 2000, gathered to hail the conquering heroes.

They cheered for all the players but they cheered most of all for Babe Ruth. The great man made a truly magnificent appearance as he stood before his worshippers on the rear platform. Stripped to his undershirt, holding a ham hock in one hand and a pitcher of beer in the other, the Babe raised both aloft in a token of acknowledgment of the reception.

"Three cheers for Babe Ruth!" cried one of the multitude, with more enthusiasm than originality.

The crowd responded with three rousing salvos and the Babe took his cue from there.

"Now three cheers for Tony Lazzeri!" bellowed the Babe throwing his arms around the second baseman.

"And now three cheers for Lou Gehrig!" cried the Babe, as the echo of the Lazzeri applause died down.

It was then that Babe had an inspiration. He gestured with ham hock and beer pitcher for silence.

"And now, folks, wotta ya say for three big cheers for my good friend Al Smith? Let's go now!" roared Ruth. This, remember, was in October, 1928, just as the Smith-Hoover presidential campaign was getting a full head of steam.

There was a silence from the assembled Hoosiers which could have been cut with a knife, although the chances are that if Babe had a knife it would have been something other than the silence he would have cut.

The Babe, still with ham hock and beer on high, gazed at the crowd in astonishment.

"If that's the way you feel, t'hell with you!" he roared and stalked off the rear platform. He may have been campaigning in what already was a lost cause but Ruth was at least forthright.

Babe made one other political gesture for Smith and it made little appreciable progress toward putting a brown derby on the wardrobe shelf in the White House. He appeared on a radio broadcast with Lazzeri. Ruth stressed his friendly feelings toward the Democratic nominee and said that not only he, but all sportsmen and athletes, were for Smith. Everybody was for Al.

"For instance," said Babe into the microphone as he threw an arm about Lazzeri's shoulders, "here's Tony Lazzeri. Now, Tony, who are the Wops going to vote for?"

Democratic leaders always felt that that speech of Ruth's gave Herbert Hoover a higher percentage of the Italian-American vote than he was entitled to.

Ruth's last appearance as a political polemicist was in 1944 when he spoke in favor of Thomas E. Dewey when the New York governor ran against Franklin D. Roosevelt. Newspapers which never before held Babe in high esteem as a political analyst gravely printed his statement that it was "time for a change." Subsequently these same papers buried on a rear page the news that it was Babe's first vote and that he had to take a literacy test before he was permitted to register.

Asking Babe to appear on a dais and say a few words was something like buying a ticket in the Irish Sweepstakes. You never knew what to expect. The New York Baseball Writers' Dinner one year happened to coincide with Ruth's birthday, or at least his accepted natal anniversary, February 7. The Hillerich and Bradsby Co., manufacturers of the Louisville Slugger bats, presented a silver bat to Ruth. It was an impromptu presentation and Babe was called from the floor to the dais to accept. Somebody in the crowd cried "Speech! Speech!" and the only way this enthusiast could have thrown a greater scare into the toastmaster was if he had cried "Fire!" The fun was on.

Ruth surveyed his audience. It was made up, as it usually is, of about equal parts of current baseball writers and ball players and of old timers. This was 1938, the occasion of Babe's forty-third or forty-fourth birthday, depending upon which version you took.

"You know what I call this dinner?" began Ruth. "I call this the 'I Wonder Dinner.' I come here every year and I wonder who'll be missing each year. I wonder who'll be missing next year? (Pointing to Colonel Ruppert and Ed Barrow) I wonder if Jake and Ed will be here next year? (Pointing to Commissioner Landis, who was alongside him on the dais) I wonder if this old goat will be here next year?"

Babe went on in that vein, a mixture of sentimentality and fatalism, a speech which had the majority of the audience in howls of appreciative laughter, but which had the older members of the congregation making mental appointments with cardiac specialists.

Joe Williams, executive sports editor of the Scripps-Howard newspapers, has reason to remember the dynamite which could be concealed in one of Ruth's impromptu orations. As a promotional stunt for the New York *World-Telegram,* Joe devised a contest to pick the most valuable scholastic player in the city. The highlight of the affair was a pep meeting, at which the schoolboys, their fans and their parents, were addressed by leading baseball lights.

This particular meeting was in 1929 at City College. The auditorium was packed when Ruth strode to the center of the stage. He hadn't had a particularly good afternoon at the Stadium and had been heckled by some bleacherites. He chose as his text, the unmannerly behavior of the fans.

"Some fans think because you're wearing a monkey suit, they can call you anything they please," began the Babe. "They don't care who is sitting next to them or what kind of names they call you. Well, I'm not going to take it any more. The next time one of these bums yells something at me, especially if he has kids sitting near him, I'm going into the stands after him and I'm going to grab that white-livered loafer by the neck and I'm going to say to him, 'Lissen, you—' "

Here the Babe paused for rhetorical effect and those with him on the dais bowed their heads, waiting for the lightning to strike from on high. American League president Ernest S. Barnard bowed as though in silent prayer. Williams put his face in his hands. Dan Daniel and myself bowed lowest of all, because we had brought the Babe. Then Ruth resumed his Philippic.

"I'm going to say to him," continued the Babe, " 'Lissen you dag-gone wise guy, who do you think you are?' "

Ruth seated himself amid thunderous applause. You could have heard Joe Williams exhale in relief two blocks away.

8

The Yankee Legend

In their one year under Bob Shawkey, the Yankees could never quite untrack themselves. The death of Miller Huggins near the close of the 1929 season had a disorganizing effect on the team. The Athletics had crashed through to the pennant and a spectacular World Series victory. Stocks had tumbled and the Yankees were tumbling with them.

One day early in this 1930 season, Waite Hoyt, a Yankee by instinct and tradition, gazed moodily up and down the Yankee bench. Some writer had asked him what he thought was the reason for the club not being in the thick of the pennant fight.

"The trouble with the Yankees this year is that they haven't enough Yankees on the team," answered Hoyt gloomily.

Waite was quite correct in his judgment. There weren't enough Yankees on that 1930 team, as the term Yankees was understood around the American League. Hoyt wasn't drawing any verbal Mason-Dixon line. He had no reference to what section of the country the players comprising the Yankee squad had come from but was merely making a frank appraisal of their outlook on baseball.

Hoyt had been on six Yankee pennant winners, three World's Champions. The Yanks, with Hoyt, had been the aristocrats of baseball. Baseball was as much of a sport to them as big game hunting to

Keystone

Frank Baker, first of the home run kings, and the daddy of 'em all, the one and only Babe. They were the backbone of the first of the many "Murderers' Rows" with which the Yanks were to plague the opposition.

a titled Englishman. It also was a profession, and a profitable one, to them, but they loved to win as much for the sheer joy of winning as for what it brought them in dollars and cents. Waite, more articulate by far than the average baseball player, or baseball writer, realized that he was seeing the end of an era.

There are really two Yankee dynasties or perhaps one dynasty divided into two parts. From the time Ed Barrow came to New York until Larry MacPhail purchased the club, the Yanks won fourteen pennants and ten World's Championships in a period of twenty-five years. Six of these were won under Huggins, eight of them under McCarthy, all of them under Barrow. Babe Ruth, as was fitting, bridged the gap, playing in seven of the fourteen Yankee World Series.

The Yankees of Huggins and the Yankees of McCarthy were widely different in their composition, even though Joe inherited several of the players from Hug's championship teams. The only thing the two squads had in common was complete domination of their field. The Huggins Yankees were swashbuckling ball players, those of McCarthy cold perfectionists.

As the Yanks went on under McCarthy to win seven pennants in eight seasons, missing the other by only two games, their rivals around the American League commented more than once upon their business-like efficiency. It was suggested that a sign could be placed in front of the Yankee dugout, a sign familiar to motorists all over the country—"Men At Work."

What both groups had, in addition to their dominance of the field, was Barrow in the front office and a fine, fierce pride in their team. To all of them, from the team of 1921 to that of 1943, the name Yankees was synonymous with champions. Players who came to the Yanks from the minors, or were obtained in trades with other major league clubs, quickly caught this winning spirit or else were traded.

Baseball wasn't just a day's work to the Yankees, either to the gay, carefree Yankees of the 20's or those who won for McCarthy. There was something personal to it. It meant something to be a Yankee, it meant something to be a winner. From Roger Peckinpaugh to Phil Rizzuto, from Wally Schang to Bill Dickey, the stamp of class was upon them. They would die rather than admit it, but they had plenty of the old school spirit and the old college try. They were Yankees because they won, they won because they were Yankees.

You never saw a Yankee on the field in Barrow's reign who didn't look like a ball player. They never got around to the individualities of baseball costume which players on other clubs affected. Their baseball flannels were simple to the point of austere severity. And the great majority of them had class off the field, too. Just as John McGraw once banned caps among the Giants, so did Joe McCarthy ban polo shirts among the Yankees.

Huggins and McCarthy were different types, yet strangely alike. Both preferred the background. Each knew baseball and ball players and nobody yet has had any extended success as a manager without knowing both. They were technicians as well as tacticians, could help a young ball player and find a spot for an old one. Neither Hug nor Joe ever was any great shakes as a hitter, yet they managed the greatest power teams in all baseball history.

Babe Ruth played on only the first of McCarthy's eight pennant winners, the 1932 team. It was Babe's last World Series and he made it one of his most spectacular. Indeed, the Series was concluded with a flourishing gesture that was in keeping with the best of Yankee tradition.

The Yanks won the first two games from the Cubs in 1932, won them in Yankee Stadium with a minimum of difficulty. They went into Chicago for the next three games, with the sixth and seventh to be played back at the Stadium if necessary. They made it three straight by taking the opener in Chicago, the game in which Babe called his shot against Charley Root. That was on a Saturday and the Cubs had to win Sunday if the Series was to continue.

Mark Roth, like Ruth a holdover from the Huggins era, was the road secretary. Mark was so conservative he wouldn't open an umbrella in a thundershower unless he had a personal O.K. from Barrow that it was raining. But old habits are hard to break. It was four years since the Yankees had been in a World Series and that Series, 1928, like the one before it, had ended in a four-straight sweep for the Yanks. What was more natural, then, that on this Saturday night in Chicago Mark should make preparations for another sweep?

Roth went the rounds of the Edgewater Beach Hotel on Chicago's lake front that night, leaving information in the room of each player and each writer. The instructions read:

"Have your bags in the lobby before you leave for the park for

Sunday's game. Pay your extras at the desk. Cabs will leave from the park for the train immediately after the game."

It never occurred to Mark that the Cubs might win the fourth game and delay the departure until Monday. It apparently never occurred to the Yankees, either, and certainly not to the Cubs. It was all over Sunday night.

There is a tendency on the part of many of those in a position to know to acclaim the 1927 Yankees as the greatest of all the Yankee teams. It always used to get Ruth's vote and it always got Barrow's, too. It was quite a club, winning 110 games and losing forty-four. It beat out the second-place Athletics by a cool nineteen games. Ruth hit his sixty home runs that season and Gehrig batted in 175 runs.

Figures, unless they're in the front line of a musical, are usually boring, but the figures on the 1927 Yankees are worth repeating: They scored almost a thousand runs (975), belted 158 homers. Gehrig batted .373, Bob Meusel was low man in the outfield with .337, as both Ruth and Combs batted .356. Tony Lazzeri hit .309, Mark Koenig, who batted .500 in the World Series against the Pirates was clocked at .285 and Jumping Joe Dugan hit .269. Pat Collins, who shared the catching with Johnny Grabowski and Bennie Bengough, batted .275. Just by way of emphasizing its all-around class, the club beat the Browns twenty-one straight times.

Huggins used only four pitchers in the Series against Pittsburgh, Hoyt (22-7), Pennock (19-8), Moore (19-7) and Pipgras (10-3). Urban Shocker, who didn't appear in the Series, had an 18-6 record. Perhaps the most remarkable feature of this pitching staff was the excellent relief hurling of Moore, a bald-headed rookie from the Sally League, who appeared in fifty games for the Yankees and had an earned run average of 2.28.

The 1927 Series was the one which the Yankees are generally credited with winning before it began. The games opened in Pittsburgh and when the Yanks arrived at Forbes Field they put on one of the most awesome exhibitions of slugging ever seen. Ruth, Gehrig, Meusel and Lazzeri hit balls out of sight, while the Pirates sat in the dugout gaping with open-mouthed wonder. There are those who maintain that just by looking at the batting drill of the Yankees, the Pirates lost all hope.

Oddly enough, despite the fact that the Yankees completed the regular American League season with a team batting average of .307, it was pitching which won the Series for them. There were only two home runs, both by Ruth, and the winning run in the last game came over with two out in the ninth by means of a wild pitch.

The very fact that pitching, rather than slugging, won the Series for the Yankees serves only to stress that the 1927 club was one which had everything. It was such members of the 1927 club as he could locate whom Barrow assembled for Lou Gehrig Day at Yankee Stadium a dozen years later. Ed, never much for sideshows or extracurricular hokum, thought that Gehrig, and the fans, would like to see the members of that great team assembled again. As a matter of fact, Ed felt like taking another look at those chaps himself.

All of the traits which were predominant in other great Yankee clubs, whether those managed by Huggins or by McCarthy, were present in generous profusion in that 1927 collection of window-breakers. The 1927 edition of the Bombers had that trait of pounding to a pulp the club it had to beat. This has been an old Yankee trick through the years, to beat off competition by literally stifling it under a flock of hits and runs.

The Yankees the year before had won the pennant rather handily from Cleveland. Late in September the two clubs met in a series in Cleveland which opened with a double header. To have any chance of catching the Yanks at all, the Indians had to win this double header. The Yankees won both games by resounding scores, causing John Kieran, current savant of Information Please, but then a baseball writer, to wire back to the New York *American:* "Paraphrasing Commodore Perry at the Battle of Lake Erie, 'We have met the enemy and where are they?' "

All this, of course, was water on the Babe's wheel. He loved being on top and the Yankees in those days were top dog most of the time. They gave the impression of being unbeatable, even in practice. In fact, they were unbeatable, even in practice, as the Dodgers used to discover when they came north with them each spring, to collect as thorough a belaboring as ever fell to the lot of any major league ball club.

The first great test of the Yankees came in 1928. There was a let-down after the big doings of 1927 and the Athletics, amazingly rebuilt by Connie Mack after years as doormats of the American League, weren't fooling this time. Even though Connie's '27 club had been left far behind by the Yankees, it was good enough to win ninety-one games. And the A's were much stronger in 1928, while the Yanks began to slide back to meet the field.

At one time in 1928, the Yankees were in front by seventeen games but then came the crack-up. Urban Shocker became ill and left the club, going home to die before the season was over. Herb Pennock, who had a perfect game going until there was one out in the eighth inning in the 1927 World Series, pitched a splendid fourteen-inning game against the White Sox and came out of it with a sore arm, to be of no help to the team for the rest of the season, even though he resorted to the most outlandish remedies such as permitting bees to

Acme

The Lip breaks in at the top. Leo Durocher poses with Ruth after joining the Yankees for his first major league job.

sting his arm in an effort to resuscitate it. Stan Coveleskie couldn't pitch at all and retired to brood in his native Shamokin, Pennsylvania, after he had won five and lost one for the Yankees. Cy Moore, the sensation of '27, split eight decisions.

There was trouble in the infield, too. Tony Lazzeri began to have the miseries and was frequently spelled by a brash youngster, Leo Durocher, who was nicknamed the Lip by his teammates. Joe Dugan, the agile jumping jack, lost much of his agility and had to call on Gene Robertson for help. It was rough going and even the seventeen-game lead wasn't enough to stand off the rush of the White Elephants from Philadelphia.

The blow fell in September. On the 7th, Washington came to Yankee Stadium and gave the Hugmen a real Black Friday, whaling them in a double header by the unlikely scores of 11 to 0 and 6 to 1. The same day the A's won a double header at Fenway Park and tied the Yankees for the lead.

Ruth hit a home run the next day to help beat Washington, but the Mackmen won another double header from the helpless Red Sox and took the American League lead by a half-game margin and moved into Yankee Stadium for a Sunday double header. It looked as though this was indeed the end of the Yankees.

If it was to be a wake, however, the Yankees had fine weather for it and an amazing crowd. In fact, the crowd was so amazing that it beguiled Barrow into giving out false attendance figures. Cousin Ed blandly announced that there were 85,265 spectators at the double header, a most improbable figure and one Ed could have reached only by counting those on the surrounding rooftops, those who had been turned away and those who had thought about coming but had changed their minds. It was, however, a large crowd, probably close to 75,000.

This, if ever, was the time for the Yanks to crack. They had dissipated a seventeen-game lead on the field, they were beset with lame arms and even the magic of a game-winning homer by Ruth the day before hadn't kept them on top. The Yanks, however, didn't crack. George Pipgras pitched a 5 to 0 shutout against the venerable John Picus Quinn in the opener, and in the second game Hoyt and Rommel were hooked up in a 3 to 3 tie when Bob Meusel broke the deadlock in typical Yankee fashion by belting a home run into the left field stands with the bases loaded. The Yanks were back in first place with a lead of a game and a half.

There was no game the day after this explosion but, in the third game of the series, young Henry Johnson stepped out and beat Lefty Grove by 5 to 3, the Yanks coming from behind on a homer by Ruth. The A's took the last game, when Orwoll outlasted Hoyt to win by 4 to 3, but the pennant boat already had left by then and the Yankees were aboard. They went west to protect the game and a half lead, winning the pennant by two and a half games and belting the Cardinals four straight in the World Series. It was a glorious comeback for the Yankees—and it also was the last shot in the barrel for the Yanks of the Huggins era. They never won again.

Usually the collapse of a great athletic machine, be it a football team or a heavyweight champion, catches everybody by surprise, especially those closest to it. Nobody learns about the "hollow shell" until it is too late. This was not the case with Huggins and his Yankees. The little Miller knew the jig was up before any of the players or the writers traveling with the team had even a hint of what was coming.

When the Athletics got away winging in 1929, none of the Yankee personnel was terribly concerned. They'd thrown away a seventeen-game lead and come from behind to take 'em the year before, hadn't they? And that was in September. Hell, this was only May. What was the use of worrying?

Even though it was only May, Hug was worrying. In fact, he was almost past the worrying stage and was resigned to what fate had in store for his ball club. Late in May, the Yankees were rained out of a game in Cleveland and Gordon Cobbledick, of the Cleveland *Plain Dealer,* came around to the Hollenden Hotel to interview Hug on the pennant race. I was in Hug's room on an entirely different matter, to get his permission to have Babe Ruth present at the *World-Telegram's* scholastic baseball rally, an incident already discussed.

Cobbledick asked Huggins if he thought the Yankees would soon snap out of it and set sail after the Athletics. Hug puffed contemplatively for some seconds, apparently deliberating upon his reply, and then spoke slowly and with no particular show of emotion, considering the nature of what he had to say.

"No, Mr. Cobbledick, I don't think the Yanks are going to catch the Athletics," answered Huggins calmly. "I don't think these Yankees are going to win any more pennants, or at least not this one. They're getting older and they're becoming glutted with success. They've been in three World Series in a row, remember, and they won the last two Series in four straight.

Keystone

The last of Miller Huggins' championship teams, the 1928 Yankees.

"They've been getting fairly high salaries and they've taken a lot of money out of baseball, a whole lot of money. They have stock market investments and these investments are giving them excellent returns at the moment. When they pick up a newspaper now, they turn to the financial page first and the sports page later. Those things aren't good for a ball club, not a ball club which is trying to beat a club like the one Mr. Mack has."

It was a startling interview, remarkable for its frankness and amazing for its prophecy. I never heard any other manager in baseball come out flat-footedly and make such a declaration about his team at such an early stage in the pennant race. Nor analyze the situation so exactly. Everything which Hug said came to pass, even though the little Miller didn't live to see it. He died, practically in harness, in the closing weeks of the 1929 season and the Athletics went on to win that pennant by eighteen games over the second place Yankees. And they went on to make it three straight pennants, until the Yankees, considerably altered by Joe McCarthy, put a stop to it in 1932.

The pride that the Yankees took in their work was shared by the pride Barrow took in their achievements. And the rough riding, hell-for-leather Cardinals gave the Yanks a kick in their pride in the 1942 World Series, the like of which neither Barrow nor the Yanks had sustained since the 1929 collapse. That was the year when the Yanks won the first game rather easily, despite a ninth-inning collapse by Red Ruffing, who at one stage seemed on his way to a no-hitter. And they never won another game, the Cards taking the next four straight, the last three of them at the Stadium.

The Yanks had been overwhelming favorites for that Series but, when they met again in 1943, the Cardinals were top dog. McCarthy's men won the opener at the Stadium, lost the second when Mort Cooper turned in a remarkable pitching job, then won the third, also played in New York, on the strength of a clutch double by Bill Johnson. They went out to St. Louis and took two straight from the Cards on their home grounds to recapture the World's Championship.

I shall never forget walking down the ramp of the Stadium with Barrow and a couple of other writers after Johnson's hit with the bases filled had given the Yanks a two-to-one edge in the Series. Groundkeepers were hosing down the Stadium turf, the fans had long since departed and the towering stands were starkly bare. There was no sound in the huge baseball plant save the clicking of telegraph and typewriter keys in the press box and the gentle swish of the hose as it sprayed the infield.

Barrow looked at the scene for a couple of long moments before he resumed his trek down the ramp. Then, to no one in particular, Ed remarked, "We'll beat those guys in St. Louis. They'll never win another game from us."

When we reached St. Louis the next day, there was a rumor that Barrow had been stricken ill and removed to a hospital and that his condition was such that he wouldn't even be allowed to follow the progress of the games by radio. This grapevine report was subsequently confirmed by press association dispatches from New York.

Bill Dickey won the final game in St. Louis with a two-run homer as Spud Chandler pitched an amazing ten-hit shutout. The Yankee players, not a few of whom were wartime replacements, were assembled in the clubhouse and Charley McManus, long-time superintendent of the Stadium and one of the earliest employees of the Yankee organization, read off a long phone message of congratulations to the players.

It was a message that Barrow, in the best of Yankee traditions, like Mark Roth and the baggage at the Edgewater Beach Hotel in 1932, had prepared and phoned to McManus *before* the game was over, a message anticipating the Yankee triumph. And the message had been prepared and phoned in defiance of orders from Barrow's doctor and pleas from Barrow's family.

Quite possibly it sounds corny, even melodramatic, that a man of Barrow's age, in his seventies, should have insisted on sending such a message when he was seriously ill. But Ed wanted that 1942 humiliation eradicated, not only from the records, but from his memory and the memory of the Yankees.

Four years later when Barrow was vacationing at St. Petersburg, disassociated at long last from the Yankees, I asked him about that message.

"Winning that 1943 World Series meant a lot to you, didn't it, Ed?" I asked.

"Meant a lot" grinned Barrow. "I should say it did. Probably the only reason I'm alive today."

That's how much the Yankee tradition means to the man who followed Babe Ruth to New York and saw this tradition grow.

It was Ruth, Barrow and Huggins who began the Yankee tradition, Barrow, McCarthy and DiMaggio who kept it alive, but it never had a greater advocate than Colonel Ruppert himself, who bought out his original partner, Cap Huston, in time to have the Yankees all to himself when they won their first World's Championship. It was Ruppert who was host at those lavish victory parties at the Hotel Commodore after the World Series of 1936, 1937 and 1938, even though he was unable to attend the last one because he was then at the beginning of his final illness.

Ruppert first tasted the delights of victory through the blasts of

Ruth's bat and he was a Yankee fan, as well as the Yankee owner, in the true Ruthian fashion. He considered the game interesting in direct proportion to the number of runs the Yankees scored. He'd sooner see the Yankees win 20 to 2 any day than he would see them win 1 to 0. In fact, the Colonel was a little suspicious of those low-score victories, as though he weren't sure that they counted as much in the league standings as the plasterings the Yankees inflicted from time to time upon their hapless opponents.

The Yankee tradition, as engendered by Ruth, fostered by Barrow and enjoyed by Ruppert, wasn't a bad one at all. Boiled down, its slogan was: Win as many as you can, by as much as you can.

9

The Beau Geste

Mark Koenig was a nice guy. He also had been a Yankee, although the two aren't necessarily incompatible. Everybody on the Yankees thought it was a nice thing when they heard the Cubs had rescued Mark from the minors in 1932 and that Mark had in turn whacked out some important base hits, including a homer, in the last month of the season to win that pennant for the Cubs.

The Yankees, however, were astonished and indignant when they learned that the Cubs were not repaying Koenig whack for whack. When it came time to divide the World Series shares, Mark was kissed off with a half-portion. Rogers Hornsby, who had managed the club until August 2 of that year when he was bounced in favor of Charley Grimm, was turned off without a nickel.

Thus, when the Cubs filed through the Yankee dugout to open the Series at the Stadium, the Yanks were ready for them and in fine voice. Koenig was the fourth or fifth Chicago player up the steps and Babe Ruth, remembering a name for a change, boomed out this greeting:

"Hi ya, Mark! Who are those cheap-skate, nickel-nursing so-and-so's with you?"

That started it and, from there on in, the Yankees never let up. It probably was a great source of personal satisfaction to Joseph Vincent McCarthy, who had been turned adrift by the Cubs two years before and now was coming back against them in the first of the eight World Series in which he was to pilot the Yankees. There was no great love lost between McCarthy and the powers that be in the Chicago front office. It was, more than is usual in a World Series, a personal battle, a grudge fight.

The Yankees, as was their wont against National League competition, won the first two games in New York without any great trouble. When they detrained at the La Salle Street station in Chicago they found a mob of several thousand milling about the taxis which were to take them to their hotel. It was, by and large, a strange crowd, more curious than hostile. It was a larger crowd than ever had met the Yankees at the train in any city, including New York. The mob neither booed nor cheered, saving their hostility for the next day at Wrigley Field.

It was in this 1932 Series that ghost-writing bloomed and flourished as never before. Ruth, of course, was top man among the sweaty literati, but McCarthy, Gehrig and several other Yanks lent their by-lines to syndicated articles. Christy Walsh, Babe's business manager and the originator of this ectoplasmic form of journalism, was known in the press box as "The Keeper of the Ghosts." Not only did he have most of the Yankees lined up, but practically all of the Cubs, from Manager Charley Grimm on down, turned expert for the Series, either for Walsh or other sponsors.

Among the specter scribes of the Cubs was Charley Root, who was to be the Chicago pitcher in the third game. Under his own by-line in the Chicago *American,* Root boldly mapped out his plan of pitching strategy against the Yankees as well as the reason for the failure of two confrères, Guy Bush and Lon Warneke, in the games in New York.

"They were too careful," was the gist of the article under Charley's name in the *American.* "The way to pitch to the Yankees is not to be over-awed by their reputations but to throw caution to the winds."

Old Caution-to-the-Winds Root was to learn early in the third game that discretion was definitely the better part of valor when it came to pitching to the Yankees.

When the Yankees trotted out on the field to take practice before the third game, the Cub rooters rose in righteous indignation. Lemons were showered on the field, particularly in left where Ruth was to perform. Lemons were tossed at the Babe and Gehrig when they took their turn at the plate. Whatever awe the gaping thousands had shown at the La Salle Street station the day before had been entirely dissipated by the blasts in the Chicago papers about the horrid New Yorkers.

In the very first inning, it looked as though Root's newly acquired nickname of Caution-to-the-Winds would have to be changed to Home-Early-Root, for the Yanks tied into him for three runs, all as the result of a first inning home run by the Bambino. By now the huge crowd of 49,986 was seriously considering throwing what lemons were left at Root and the Cubs.

Keystone

Just before the called shot. Ruth crossing the plate after his first inning three-run homer against Charley Root in the third game of the 1932 World Series at Wrigley Field. Earl Combs already has scored and Joey Sewell pauses to shake the Bam's hand. Lou Gehrig is waiting to hit and Gabby Hartnett is the Cub catcher. Roy Van Graflan is the umpire.

However, the Cubs made a battle out of this one, for a while at least. They came back to tie the score at 4 to 4 against George Pipgras, who made World Series history of a dubious, if not downright negative, sort in that game by striking out five times.

Came the fifth and Root was still in there. When the Babe came to bat those Cub fans who had hoarded their citrus ammunition pegged a few lemons in the direction of the big fellow. The Chicago players, who had been taking an awful verbal shellacking during the Series, most of it from Ruth, cut loose on him. The Cubs themselves were not without players who were gifted at the dodge of riding the opposition and they gave Ruth what-for in no uncertain terms.

The net result of this was the most defiant, and the most debated, gesture in World Series history. Root threw a called strike past the Babe and the Cub bench let the big fellow have it. Babe, holding the bat in one hand, held up the index finger of the other, to signify that it was indeed a strike. Root threw another called strike. Ruth held up two fingers and the Cub bench howled in derision.

It was then the big fellow made what many believe to be the beau geste of his entire career. He pointed in the direction of dead center field. Some say it was merely a gesture toward Root, others that he was just letting the Cub bench know that he still had the big one left. Ruth himself has changed his version a couple of times but the reaction of most of those who saw him point his finger toward center field is that he was calling his shot.

Whatever the intent of the gesture, the result was, as they say in Hollywood, slightly colossal. Ruth hit the ball on a line into the center field bleachers, the farthermost point in the park. It broke the tie and it also broke the back of the Cubs, particularly when Gehrig followed with another smashing homer. The ball game, like caution, had been thrown to the winds.

Ruth's homer in this game, the last of the fifteen he was to hit in World Series play, was one of his best. It traveled on a low trajectory all the way. When it first left the bat I thought Billy Herman, at second base, had a chance to catch the line drive but it took off before it ever reached him and sailed into the bleachers directly under the Wrigley Field scoreboard. There's an ivy-covered brick wall there now, as the park has been remodeled since, with a 400-foot marker at about where Ruth's hit cleared the wire fence of the old bleachers.

Warren Brown, Chicago sports historian, claims that seven different fans were found outside Wrigley Field after the game, each proudly exhibiting the ball with which Ruth had called his shot. There was a great dispute as to where the ball had actually landed, but my vote goes to a ticket seller, who was cooped in a small booth under the scoreboard, selling bleacher seats. He claimed the ball landed in his booth. It was hard to follow the ball because of the trick background at Wrigley Field but, in trying to determine where it landed, I saw no scurrying among the fans for possession of the souvenir, such as usually occurs when a home run is hit into the stands. It is for this reason that I believe the chap in the ticket booth. The ball didn't leave the park and his claim that it landed in his booth would account for the absence of a scuffle among the fans.

After the game it was unanimously accepted by writers, fans and players that Ruth had called his shot against Root. In fact, when somebody asked the Babe how he would have felt if he had fanned after making his defiant gesture, he replied:

"I never thought of that. I'd have looked like an awful chump, wouldn't I?"

Late that winter, at a dinner given by Christy Walsh at the New York Athletic Club for his All-America Board, Ruth declared that calling his shot against Root was the biggest thrill he had ever had in baseball. As time went on, however, there was a general move to discount the big fellow's gesture and in the general debate which followed Babe himself grew confused and wasn't certain whether he had picked out a spot in the bleachers to park the ball, was merely pointing generally to the outfield or was signaling that he still had one swing to go.

Emily Post to the contrary, everybody agrees that Babe did point in the direction of center field and that he did hit a home run there and that's good enough for me.

Defiant, even erratic, gestures were nothing new for the big fellow. In 1930 when he hit three home runs at Shibe Park for the first time in an American League game, he came up in the ninth inning with a chance to make it four and, for reasons best known to himself, took a right-handed stance at the plate. Since the pitcher was the ancient spitballer, Jack Quinn, a right-hander, Babe didn't even have the excuse that he was playing the percentage.

Here was Babe with a chance to make new and startling baseball history. Nobody had hit four home runs in a game since big Ed Delahanty back in the 90's and Ruth was passing up the chance by clowning around and batting right-handed. He took two strikes against Quinn as a right-hander and then went over to the left side of the plate and struck out!

It is because of his antics that day in Shibe Park that I'm always certain Ruth was gesturing that he was going to hit the next ball out of the lot against Root. I don't think Babe had any intention of hitting it into the exact center field direction in which he was pointing, but simply was indicating that he was going to give the ball a ride. He did and then he gave the Cubs a ride as he circled the bases.

Historians build up a touching story of the first of the ten World Series in which Ruth appeared, when he pinch-batted in 1915 as a member of the Red Sox against Grover Cleveland Alexander, who had just pitched the Phillies into the first pennant they had ever won. And, so far, the only one. It also was the first Series appearance for Alex and the historians would have you believe that Old Pete made a sucker out of the Babe, since he had a fruitless turn at bat.

Ruth went to bat against Alexander in the ninth inning of the first game with the Sox behind 3 to 1 and a man on first as the result of an error by Fred Luderus, Philly first baseman. The Babe, probably aiming for the short fence at Baker Bowl, pulled the ball viciously down the first base line and Luderus made a brilliant play to smother it for a putout.

The Babe, as all who knew him will testify, had a way with him. The bigger the crowd, the bigger the Babe. It was only natural therefore that some of his greatest achievements, such as the home run against Root, should come in World Series competition. Ruth was a money player and had the true star's ability to rise to the situation. He made all sorts of plays in his Series career, brilliant in all of them save the 1922 flopperoo against the Giants. In his last five World Series, of which the Yankees won four, the big fellow hit a total of fourteen home runs.

One of Ruth's greatest World Series plays, oddly enough, was not made with a bat. It was the catch which ended the 1928 Series in St. Louis, when a crippled Yankee team upset the highly favored Cardinals in four straight games, a most surprising form reversal. After a ding-dong battle in the fourth game, with the Cardinals going into the top of the seventh with a 2 to 1 bulge, the Yanks asserted themselves and swept into the lead. In the ninth, with two on and two out, Frankie Frisch came to bat for the Cards.

Owner Sam Breadon had built extra field boxes for the Series, which took up most of the space in foul territory at Sportsman's Park, making it almost impossible to catch a foul fly. Ruth had gone into the Series with what he somewhat inelegantly termed "a bum gam" and was limping more noticeably than ever now, as the fourth game drew to a close. There is little doubt that Miller Huggins would have replaced Babe with a younger outfielder as a precautionary defensive move after the Yanks had gone ahead, except that Hug was plumb out of outfielders, young or old. Earl Combs was confined to pinch-hitting roles because of a broken finger and Ben Paschal already had been relieved in center by Cedric Durst, so the little Miller had to stick with Babe in left.

With two on, two out and one Cardinal run already in, it looked as though Hoyt was in for a rough ninth when Frisch lofted a high foul along the left field line, with Babe in hobbling pursuit. Ruth was running parallel to the field boxes with his right and gloved hand next to the foul line. Into a blizzard of flying scorecards and newspapers, the big fellow made one swish with his famous white glove, picked the ball out of the chin-whiskers of an astonished St. Louisan and kept right on hobbling toward the exit through the third base dugout of the Cardinals, his hand held triumphantly aloft with the ball in his glove. The game, and the Series, was over.

It was in this same Series that Ruth compiled his best blue ribbon record. He batted .625, made ten hits in the four games, three of which were homers which he hit in the last game, the game he ended with his spectacular catch. And among these three homers was the famous "quick-pitch" home run against Wee Willie Sherdel, a blow which is among the most historical of Ruth's Series home runs.

This particular Series was one in which the Cardinals were humiliated, which in itself is unique because the Gas Housers usually manage to give a most excellent account of themselves when playing for the blue chips. They had been routed in the first three games by scores of 4 to 1, 9 to 3 and 7 to 3 and were really making a go of it in the fourth game, behind the courageous pitching of Sherdel.

The Cards were in front by 2 to 1 when Ruth came to bat in the seventh. Sherdel got two strikes on the big fellow. He took Earl Smith's return after the second strike and whipped it to the plate without a windup for what the crowd thought was the third strike. While the fans were still roaring their approval, Cy Pfirman, National League umpire working behind the plate, ruled it was a quick-pitch and no strike. This was in accordance with the instructions issued to the umpires before the Series by Commissioner Landis that the quick pitch would be barred.

Sherdel, Smith, Frisch and Manager Bill McKechnie stormed around Pfirman but he stood his ground, as was to be expected. Ruth stood by grinning, waiting for play to be resumed. When it was, he hit the first pitch into the stands for a homer, his second, to tie up the game at 2 to 2. Then Lou Gehrig followed with an even longer drive and the Yanks were in front, there to stay. In the next inning, Ruth and Alexander faced each other for the last time in a World Series and the Babe blasted his third home run of the day.

This, by the way, was the second time Ruth had hit three home runs in a World Series game and in the same ball park. The big fellow had belted three in the fourth game of the 1926 Series. He hit two off Flint Rhem in his first two shots at that rugged Carolinian and the third off Herman Bell. One of Babe's homers, hit on a three-and-two pitch, was the longest hit ever made at Sportsman's Park, a drive which carried well up into the center field bleachers.

In the seventh game of this Series, Ruth hit another home run and he ended this game, and the Series, in a manner which caused almost as much discussion as his catch in 1928 was to cause two years later. This was the game in which Alexander, a winner the day before, came out of the bull pen to save the day for the Cards by fanning Tony Lazzeri with the bases filled in the seventh and the Red Birds ahead by 3 to 2. Old Pete set the Yankees down in order in the eighth and got rid of Combs and Koenig to open the ninth. Up came Ruth, who walked on a three-two pitch, his eleventh pass of the Series. With Bob Meusel at the plate, Ruth took it into his head to steal second and Bob O'Farrell nailed him with a throw to Hornsby. Nobody had given Ruth the steal sign and nobody, to this day, knows why he went down to extermination for the final out of the Series. He probably got tired standing around.

Those who remember Ruth in his World Series days with the Yankees when he was hitting everything but women and little children will be surprised to learn that he made only one hit in the three Series which he played as a member of the Red Sox and that that hit wasn't a homer. It was merely a triple. The blow was hit in the 1918 Series, the last Babe was to appear in as a Boston player.

Ed Barrow, managing the 1918 Bosox,. had opened the Series with the Babe and he had shut out the Cubs, 1 to 0, in Chicago. Babe made his second start in the fourth game at Fenway Park, Boston, and Bar-

Keystone

The Babe at the height of his pitching career with the Red Sox.

row must have had a hunch. He had been using Ruth a great deal as a pinch-hitter that season and the big fellow had bettered .300 and had hit eleven home runs which total, believe it or not, had tied him for the American League home run crown with Tilly Walker, Philadelphia outfielder.

At any rate, when it came time to start Ruth in the fourth game, Barrow batted him in sixth place, the only time in history a starting pitcher in a World Series batted anywhere in the batting order except last. The Babe was followed by the third baseman, shortstop and catcher. This was the game in which the Bam ran his string of consecutive scoreless World Series innings to twenty-nine, a feat which will be dealt with later on in this chapter. Right now the issue is the first of the forty-two hits Ruth was to make as a World Series competitor.

George Tyler and Ruth southpawed their way up to the fourth without a run. The Sox got two on, with two out, against Tyler when Ruth came to bat. The first three pitches to Babe were wide but then George slipped in a slow curve on which Ruth took a lusty but futile swipe. The next was called a strike but, when Tyler tried to burn the third one by, the big Bam proved for the first time that he was death on those three-and-two pitches. He leathered the ball far into right field, over Max Flack's head, for a triple, scoring two runs that turned out to be mighty important in the 3 to 2 victory of the Red Sox. Such is the story of the Babe's first World Series hit, a harbinger of things to come.

The Cubs finally broke through Babe's service in this game to tie it up at 2 to 2 in the eighth, the first runs scored against Ruth after twenty-nine innings of Series pitching. Boston went ahead in its half of the eighth and Joe Bush pitched the ninth, while Babe played left field. That was another Series distinction for Ruth, to start a game as a pitcher and finish it as an outfielder.

It has often been stated, and frequently by no less an authority than Ruth himself, that the record of which the big fellow is most proud among the dozens he holds is his record for scoreless innings in the World Series. I have heard Ruth refer to it with pride more often than I have heard him mention any of his other achievements. As a matter of fact, the Babe never talked much of any of his records, such as the sixty home runs he blasted in 1927. He was much more likely to recall the amusing aspect of some home run, rather than its place in baseball's archives. He never, however, kidded about the twenty-nine scoreless innings he pitched against the Cubs and Dodgers in the Series of 1916 and 1918.

It is quite possible that Babe was enamored of this distinction above all others because of professional pride, because while pitching he had been regarded as strictly a thrower, which is the trade's term for one who pitches with more brawn than brain. To be honest about it, Ruth was a thrower—and what a thrower!

It is unlikely that any pitcher made a more inauspicious World Series debut than George Herman Ruth did in that second game of the 1916 Series with the Dodgers, which was played at Braves Field. Ruth retired the first two Brooklyn batters and then Hi Myers whaled a line drive to center, which took a bad hop over Tilly Walker's head and the speedy Hi had scooted around the bases for an inside-the-park homer before the ball could be recovered. It should have been no more than a single and it was a tough break for the young left-hander but it was the only run Uncle Robby's Dodgers were to get in the ball game, which was to stretch into fourteen innings, the longest in World Series history.

The Red Sox tied it up in the third when Ruth batted in his first run in Series play, although that worthy form of endeavor was not to find its way into box scores for some years later, until Bill Hanna, crusading baseball writer for the New York *Herald Tribune,* was to force its adoption on the major leagues. After Everett Scott had tripled in the third, Ruth brought him home with an infield out, a ball Cutshaw fumbled long enough at second base to prevent a play at the plate. This was a tough break for Sherry Smith, the southpaw who was pitching against the Babe.

Those two runs, both scored by rather questionable means, were the only runs in the ball game until the fourteenth when Del Gainer hit a two-bagger into the gathering darkness to score Mike McNally and break up the great duel between the two southpaws.

After winning his first World Series game by a 2 to 1 score in fourteen rounds, Ruth never got a chance to pitch again in that Series and had to wait until the opener of the 1918 classic with the Cubs. Again the Babe drew a left-handed opponent and again the Babe covered himself with glory as he outlasted Hippo Jim Vaughn to win by 1 to 0.

Those nine scoreless rounds against the Cubs, added to the thirteen he had racked up against the Dodgers after the freak home run by Myers, made it twenty-two consecutive innings for the Babe without a run against him.

Part of Ruth's experiences in the fourth game at Fenway Park already have been related, including his fourth-inning triple against Tyler which got the Red Sox off to a two-run lead. The Cubs finally scored two in the eighth to end Ruth's string at twenty-nine. When Babe walked the first two men to face him in the ninth, Barrow yanked the left-hander and sent him to the outfield. Since the Bostons had broken the tie in their half of the eighth, Ruth was officially the winning pitcher. It was his last World Series appearance as a pitcher and the last time he played in a World Series with any club but the Yankees. For that matter, it was the last time the Red Sox were in a Series until 1946, almost thirty years later.

A peculiar pattern ran through each of Ruth's three World Series games. He started each game against a brother left-hander, Sherry Smith, Hippo Vaughn and George Tyler. The scores of all three games were close—2 to 1, in fourteen innings, 1 to 0 and 3 to 2. And Babe won them all.

There is no telling how far Ruth might have gone as a pitcher had he been an ordinary hitter. But the big fellow was no more an ordinary hitter than he was an ordinary ball player. Barrow swears the Babe was as good as any left-hander he ever saw and Ed looked at a lot of them, fellows like Pennock, Grove, Gomez and Newhouser.

Ruth's power and his reflexes were so extraordinary that he couldn't miss being a great hitter. Pennock recalls pitching a game for the Red Sox in Chicago in 1919, the year Barrow decided that the big fellow's talents were to be best utilized in the outfield.

"I was pitching against Dave Danforth, the fellow with all those trick deliveries, the shine ball and such," recalled Pennock. "It was scoreless until well along in the game. The Babe came up about the seventh or eighth and shortened up on his bat, the first time I had ever seen him do that. He was holding it about three or four inches from the end. And he whaled away at a ball and hit it on a line into the left field seats. You know what that White Sox park is like. Imagine any hitter having power enough to hit a ball to the opposite field like that, batting choked up! And batting against a guy throwing shiners

Press Association

There she goes! Ruth hitting his sixtieth home run of the 1927 season against Tom Zachary, Washington southpaw, at Yankee Stadium, a record which still stands.

and emery balls and all that. The home run, by the way, won the game for me, 1 to 0."

Ruth couldn't possibly have afforded a better example of his amazing reflexes than in the manner in which he hit his sixtieth home run in 1927 at Yankee Stadium, the homer which broke the record they said could never be broken, the record of fifty-nine he had set six years before when he had the much closer fences of the Polo Grounds to draw a bead on for the seventy-seven home games of the Yankees.

It was getting down toward the fag end of the season when Ruth hit his fifty-ninth to tie his 1921 record. Tom Zachary, a left-hander, was pitching for Washington but when the Babe was right it didn't matter from which side the pitcher delivered. They threw it and he hit it. Tom was a smooth operator, who had good stuff and a good head.

Zachary started a pitch for the plate and the Babe started his swing. As the ball neared the hitter it looked as though it was going to come in belt high and get a piece of the plate. And Ruth had started his swing to hit it under those conditions. Then the ball broke sharply, coming in a good six inches inside the plate and low and the big fellow altered his swing, which was halfway completed, to meet the change in the path of the ball. When Babe finally hit the ball, he hit it off his shoetops and golfed it into the right field bleachers for his sixtieth home run of the season.

All this, of course, happened in a split second, but try and realize the reactions and reflexes of Ruth and you'll have some idea of why he was the greatest home run hitter the game has ever known. Here he had started a swing, the object of which was to hit a ball which he expected would come over a corner of the plate about waist high and he had to change directions in mid-air, so to speak, to hit at a ball which was six inches inside and about ankle high.

For the average hitter it would have been a miracle to have hit the ball at all, or even to have been able to check his swing, but with the big fellow he not only altered the course of his swing and met the ball, but knocked it out of the park as well!

It was demonstrations like that by Ruth which made it possible for so many baseball people to understand his beau geste against Charley Root in the World Series of 1932. A batter who could follow a pitch as the Babe did Zachary's, with a record hanging in the balance, was entitled to call his shots. And darn near anytime he felt like it, too!

The First Cut

Although a Boston writer, I think it was Bill Cunningham, once maligned St. Petersburg, Florida, as "The City of the Living Dead," it is a fine resort town and one which has nurtured more pennant winners than any other spring training camp base in history. To be sure, St. Pete probably has more septuagenarians than are to be found anywhere this side of Shangri-La, and benches for them to sit upon, too, but you can't beat its climate or its fine new ball park, Al Lang Field, which was opened with appropriate dedicatory ceremonies on March 12, 1947.

Back in 1932, however, Al Lang Field was merely a gleam in the eye of the man in whose honor it was to be named fifteen years later. Exhibition games in St. Pete then were played in Waterfront Park, a dirty, wooden pavilion, littered with peanut shells, a fire trap if ever there was one. Despite its lack of appeal, Waterfront Park drew its share of baseball fans, among them a fair sprinkling of the septuagenarian tourists of whom the Boston writer had spoken so unfeelingly.

These fans, septuagenarians and even those still in their nonage, were more than a mite disappointed one blustery March Sunday in 1932 when the Yankees opened their exhibition season against the Boston Braves and there was some young rookie with the implausible name of George Selkirk playing right field in place of Babe Ruth. Joe Williams remarked in his column in the New York *World-Telegram* that "it was somewhat like putting a Wall Street runner into the president's chair in the office of J. P. Morgan & Co."

The reason for the absence of Ruth was not that it had turned out to be an unseasonable, even unusual, afternoon for St. Petersburg but that the Babe was holding out. And the Babe was holding out for the very simple reason that Colonel Ruppert and Ed Barrow, in their infinite wisdom, had decided to reduce his salary. Their excuse was that there was something abroad in the land called a "depression," which sounded like a pretty flimsy, trumped-up excuse to the big fellow, who certainly had seen no signs of one. Which was understandable enough, since it was hardly considered cricket to open soup

Keystone

Manager Joe McCarthy lets Babe and Colonel Ruppert do the talking at St. Pete in 1932. Eventually, the Colonel was to talk Ruth into taking the first salary cut of his career.

kitchens or install bread lines around golf courses or ball parks, the two places where Ruth had been spending most of his time since the bottom fell out of the market back in October, 1929.

White collar workers had been cut to the bone, the horribly misnamed Scotch Week was in force in many firms, which meant an employee worked one week each month without being paid, the equivalent of at least a twenty-five per cent salary cut. Capable workmen were selling apples on the very corners around which President Hoover had claimed prosperity was lurking. The apple sellers had strategic posts from which to greet prosperity upon its return, when and if.

For once the newspaper men covering the Yankees were not sympathetic to Ruth's holdout demands. Too many of them had received notices after they arrived in the training camp that their pay had been reduced ten per cent, with the hint that other cuts were around the corner and these future cuts would, in all probability, beat prosperity around that corner. And it didn't look like any photo finish, either.

Those writers who were closest to Ruth attempted to convince the slugger that this was no time to hold out, with millions unemployed and thousands on the point of actual starvation. How much did Babe want, anyway?

"Just what I've been getting for the last two seasons," explained Ruth with what he thought was a great show of patience, "$80,000."

"$80,000 a year! In these times!" expostulated one of the writers. "Don't be silly, Babe. Why that's more than Hoover gets for being president of the United States."

"What the hell has Hoover got to do with this?" demanded the Babe. "Anyway, I had a better year than he did."

Eventually Ruth's advisors made it plain to him that he would have to take a pay reduction. This was hard for the big fellow to see. Ever since he had come out of "The Home" in Baltimore eighteen years before, Ruth's pay had gone up from contract to contract and sometimes in mid-season. He couldn't understand why it should recede. Nevertheless, the ball player who had signed his first contract for $600 a year and had seen that annual stipend climb all the way to $80,000 had to start coming down the golden stairs he had been ascending so consistently ever since 1914.

As long as it was Ruth who was going to give in, Colonel Ruppert was willing to make a concession to the point of having the signing ceremony take place at the Jungle Club, where the Babe and Clair were making their St. Petersburg home.

It was rather a flossy affair, with the newsreel cameras grinding away and a score of still-camera men and reporters on hand. The only hitch was that none of the parties concerned could dig up a fountain pen. A friend of Ruppert's, a malt-and-hops salesman from Louisville, one Colonel Wattenberg, finally produced a pen and the Babe signed a blank contract. He had agreed to come to terms at $70,000, but I was told later that when it came time to fill in the blank spaces, Ruppert made it $72,000. Jake always liked "Root," as he called the big fellow.

Probably few of us watching the signing on the lawn of the Jungle Club that day realized it but, in seeing Babe take his first cut, we were witnesses to the first shadow across the career of the great man. Each succeeding time he signed a contract he was to take a reduction from his previous one.

Had any of us given it serious thought, it should have been fairly evident that this had to be the beginning of the end. Even though the great majority of Americans considered the depression a transient phenomenon, it should have been plain that the $80,000 the Babe had drawn in each of the seasons of 1930 and 1931 marked the high-water mark.

Ball clubs in 1932 didn't have the artificial stimulation of night games. That was just something for the bushes until Larry MacPhail came along with arc lights for Cincinnati's Crosley Field three years later. When Ruth's contract reached $80,000, it reached the saturation point. The Babe, remember, was in his late 30's by this time and his productivity figured to decline.

Although 1947 saw two other American Leaguers threaten Ruth's high-water mark in wages, actually Babe's figure seems safe for a long time to come. Remember that Babe's $80,000 in 1930 and 1931 was "take-home pay." There was neither social security nor withholding tax. And the general income tax was a great deal less, per dollar, than it is today. And there isn't any need to bring up the fact that a buck went considerably farther in those days.

To appreciate Ruth's stubborn balking at this first salary cut, you must appreciate that his salary had increased by leaps and bounds ever since the day Jack Dunn had signed the legal papers to remove Big George from St. Mary's Industrial Home for Boys. Dunn signed him to a contract calling for $100 a month and then gave him a raise before selling him to the Red Sox. Joe Lannin gave him $3500 for his first full season with the Red Sox in 1915.

By the time H. Harrison Frazee had given Lannin a lot of paper for the Red Sox and was backing musical comedies, including *No, No Nannette!* in which Louise Groody sang "Tea for Two," Ruth was getting to be a big shot. Frazee couldn't say "No, no Babe" when the big fellow yelled for more dough after the Sox had won the World Series of 1918. He finally signed Babe for $9000 and subsequently gave him another grand as a bonus during the season.

With the Yankees, of course, Ruth really moved ahead. The first step in the program was to tear up his holdover Boston contract and give him a new one at double the figure, which allowed Babe to draw down $20,000 in 1920, his first year with New York. He was boosted another $10,000 for 1921. Despite the bull-headed defiance he had shown to Judge Landis that winter, which drew him a suspension, the Yankees made Ruth the highest paid ball player of that time.

Ruth had gone to Hot Springs, Arkansas, that winter of 1921-22 to boil out at the baths and Cap Huston went down there after him and signed him to what amounted to a five-year contract at $52,000. The Babe always found the fun-loving Huston easier to do business with than the stand-offish Ruppert, but that worked both ways, for Cap could wheedle Babe into line with less trouble than his partner. The contract covered the seasons of 1922, 1923 and 1924 and gave the club the option of renewing it at the same terms for 1925 and 1926.

Despite the attendant fanfare to this contract, which stressed the point that Ruth was now the most highly rewarded player in the history of baseball, it was an excellent document for the Yankees. They had the big fellow for the next three years without the possibility of a holdout and if he continued to hit homers (and he was only 27) the club had him tied up for two additional seasons. It was shrewd manipulation by the supposedly careless and carefree Huston and probably was the smartest contract to which the Yankees ever signed Ruth.

After the 1926 World Series, in which the Cardinals beat the Yankees in seven games, Ruth continued to climb, this time with a three-

Keystone

Babe takes to the links at Hot Springs, Arkansas, after being signed to a five-year contract at $52,000 per season by Colonel Huston before the 1922 season opened.

year contract for $70,000. He then scaled the Matterhorn with the two-year contract at $80,000 and then started down the other side of the slope with another $70,000 contract, this for two years, which he signed that March afternoon at St. Petersburg's swank Jungle Club. And, incidentally, if you're going down hill, $70,000 per is a sort of graceful first step.

The next step, however, was not so graceful. It was, in Babe's own words, "a helluva bump." And it was rather craftily contrived, too. The first hint anybody had of it was when Dan Daniel sprang an exclusive story in the New York *World-Telegram* to the effect that Babe Ruth would be offered a contract calling for one year at $25,000. This was about six weeks before the 1934 training season was to start.

The announcement caused quite a hullabaloo and brought forth the usual hatful of denials but none of them from the right place. Ed Barrow and Colonel Ruppert kept significantly mum on the matter. I was working on the same paper with Daniel and he told me that he had got his information through overhearing a telephone conversation Barrow made while he, Daniel, was in Barrow's office.

"And I'm not so sure he didn't want me to overhear it, either," reported Dan.

Apparently Barrow had made no effort to keep the cut secret from Daniel. The general manager of the Yankees had then been dealing with newspaper men for over a quarter of a century and he knew well enough what the reaction of a reporter would be who overheard a phone conversation such as the one he made with Dan on the Erie.

It always has been my belief that Barrow wished Daniel to hear the phone conversation about the $25,000 offer to Ruth so that the story would be printed as a trial balloon. It was, and Ed listened attentively to the reaction and then recommended that Ruth be offered a contract for $25,000.

The Babe was furious and told reporters he'd never sign. "I don't care how much I sign for but I won't sign for $25,000 if I never play ball again," he declared. "I'm not going to make that guy Daniel look good."

Eventually the big fellow was brought into line for $35,000 and it was the last time he ever signed a contract with the Yankees. A lot of water had flowed under the bridges in two years and a great many more banks had closed their doors. It was a far cry from 1932 when

Ruth was demanding $80,000 and "compromising" for $70,000, just twice as much as his latest contract called for. There was, of course, an explanation for it. The Babe was nearing forty and he couldn't get around in the outfield any more.

It was tragic, in a way, to learn that Ruth was basing his salary demands on his drawing powers, which were as great as ever. The Babe was still box office magic. Yet he never had to resort to personal magnetism as a talking point for his salary before. The Yankees paid Ruth because he was a great ball player and made the Yankees a great ball team. Now he was bargaining like a sideshow freak.

Ruth's fight against the $25,000 contract was his last holdout battle. When he went to the National League in the spring of 1935, he signed some sort of peculiar document with Judge Emil Fuchs, which was filled with promises but short on actual cash. Years afterward, he used to maintain that the Braves owed him money, but since he never collected it, and had good legal advisors, the chances are that Babe was too quick to translate some of the Boston promises into gold.

There was always a great deal of cynicism directed toward the belated signings of the Babe when he was with the Yankees. There were many fans who were convinced that Ruth's protracted holdout battles with the management were nothing more than publicity stunts. This wasn't the case at all, since Ruth had far more publicity value signed to a Yankee contract than he did unsigned. The big fellow's publicity was always at par and there was no need to resort to artificial respiration.

It was true, however, that Ruth, when it came time for the final surrender, often signed without looking at his contract. This was because when he finally came to terms, except for his final Yankee contract, there never was much difference, relatively speaking, between what Babe was demanding and what the club was asking. And Ruth had enough native shrewdness to know that it tickled Colonel Ruppert's vanity when he signed, sight unseen. The result was that Jake might impulsively ink in a figure a thousand or two higher than the one which the Colonel had previously set as the absolute maximum. That was what happened in 1932, when the Babe signed a blank contract.

As to holding off the signing for the proper stage effects, the club would have been delighted if it could have had Ruth under signature by every Christmas. The sooner Ruth signed, the easier it was to round up the rest of the recalcitrants. Other Yankees felt encouraged to remain adamant in their demands while the big fellow was still at large. Once the Babe was brought into line, the others had little choice except to follow.

Ruth himself, of course, didn't enjoy his protracted holdout duels with the guardian watchdog of the Ruppert treasury, Mr. Edward Grant Barrow. Barrow ran the Yankees as a business and saw to it that his employer, the Colonel, did the same thing. In fact, Ed impressed this so strongly on Ruppert that the latter indignantly told Waite Hoyt at one salary conference: "Stop it, Hoyt. What do you think I am, a millionaire?" Which, of course, is precisely what he was.

Those who thought that the holdout battles were carefully calculated dodges between Ruth and Ruppert might be interested to learn some of the behind-the-scenes events leading up to the Babe's signing of his $80,000 contract at St. Petersburg in the spring of 1930, the largest contract ever signed by a ball player.

Ruth had just completed a three-year contract at $70,000 annually and he was now asking another three-year contract, this one for $85,000. Colonel Ruppert couldn't even come close to seeing eye-to-eye with Babe on that one and it looked as though this would be the most protracted of all their financial wrangles.

Dan Daniel, the same scribe who was to overhear Barrow's $25,000 offer a few years later, came close to holding a very large burlap in Babe's $80,000 deal and through no fault of any of those involved.

Daniel was peacefully making his way home from the movies in St. Petersburg one midnight and in the course of his meanderings up Central Avenue, he glanced into the office of the Western Union and discovered to his horror that a confrère was engaged in filing a story at an hour when all self-respecting baseball writers should have had their work behind them.

The industrious author was Ford Frick, since president of the National League but then a Hearst minion on the New York *Journal*. Knowing Ford to be a great hand at getting his copy out of the way early, Dan barged in and demanded to know what was up.

"I had dinner with Babe and Clair out at the Jungle Club tonight," explained Frick, "and Babe tells me he's not going to fool around

Press Association

Ruth poses in front of the Yankee dugout with the war club he wielded so effectively that it eventually brought him a two-year contract at $80,000, the highest ever received by any ball player.

any longer. He won't play in tomorrow's exhibition game against the Braves unless he is signed, because if he plays unsigned and breaks a leg or something, he'll be through. He and Clair have talked it over and if Jake doesn't sign him at his terms by noon tomorrow, he's going to turn in his uniform and go home. And he means it."

"That's quite a story," commented Daniel, "quite a story. Do you mind if I send something to the *Telegram* on it?"

"I guess it will be all right," responded Frick reluctantly, but knowing full well that wild horses couldn't keep Dan from getting the story on the wire, permission or no.

Whereupon Daniel sat down and pounded off 1500 words on the rebellion of Ruth in something like twenty-eight minutes flat, breaking his own record for the course.

The next morning, Saturday, with Ruth's ultimatum having less than two hours to go, Daniel got a phone call from his desk in New York. "Congratulations," he says they said but, knowing desks, I think he was embellishing it a bit. "You scooped the town on the story of Ruth quitting," continued the voice from New York.

"Scooped the town?" repeated Daniel incredulously. "Are you sure the *Journal* didn't have anything on it?"

"Not a line," answered New York cheerfully.

Dan wandered the streets of St. Pete pondering the mystery of what happened to Frick's story. In the course of his contemplative peregrinations he ran across Ruth himself.

"Well, Babe, what are you going to do now?" asked Daniel. It was then about 11 A.M.

"Do? Why, I am going out and play against the Braves this afternoon," answered Babe, as if playing against the Braves were the most natural thing in the world for him to do.

"But I thought you were going to quit if you weren't signed by noon," gasped Daniel. "Have you signed?"

"No," answered Ruth cheerfully, "but it's a nice, sunny day and I feel like playing ball. Besides Judge Fuchs (owner of the Braves) is a good old guy and he can use the dough."

"What about quitting?" asked Dan weakly.

"Quitting?" repeated Babe, as puzzled as though Daniel had been speaking Sanskrit. "Quitting? Oh, yeah! I see what you mean. But that was last night."

"Well, you certainly put me in a fine spot," said Dan bitterly.

"Put you in a spot?" boomed Babe. "What the hell are you talking about?"

With one eye on the clock, Daniel poured forth the story of how he had just been congratulated by his office on a scoop which wasn't going to be a scoop much longer, which, in fact, might take that year's Pulitzer prize for fake reporting. Babe was moved, but not too much.

"Wotta ya want me to do?" he demanded of Daniel.

"Quit," ordered Dan flatly. "Turn in your uniform just like you said you were going to do last night—and just like it says in the *Telegram* you're going to do today."

"Turn in my uniform?" echoed Ruth in horror-stricken tones. "Don't be silly. I couldn't do *that!*"

"Well, then, hunt up Ruppert and sign before twelve o'clock," advised Daniel. "Otherwise you'll have me looking like a mug."

"But I can't sign at $80,000," declared Ruth petulantly. "I want $85,000."

It was then that Daniel decided to explain the economic facts of life to the Babe. He told Ruth that times were tough all over, that only yesterday thousands had rioted in Union Square seeking a crust of bread. Dan told me later that he never did find out why hunger-rioters always asked for anything as unappetizing as a crust of bread and that, inasmuch as they were rioting, it always seemed silly to him that they didn't ask for something more substantial in the way of pacification. Ruth, however, seemed impressed.

"All right," he said. "Get Jake and I'll sign."

Then followed the most frenzied half-hour in Daniel's life. He led Ruth to the Princess Martha Hotel where Colonel Ruppert was stopping. Ruppert was not available. The desk clerk reported he had gone for a walk. Dan was desperate. There was no way of telling how long the big fellow would remain amenable. At any moment, Babe might decide he was being played for a sucker and walk off. And if Babe walked off, there was no telling which direction he would take. He might walk to the golf course to play eighteen holes or he might walk out to Waterfront Park and climb into his monkey-suit. And he might conceivably walk home, pack and start looking up time tables. Time, as they say, was of the essence.

Imploring Ruth to give him his sacred word of honor that he

wouldn't leave the lobby of the Princess Martha, Daniel set off to track down Ruppert. He found the Colonel walking the shores of Mirror Lake with his companion-in-arms, the ubiquitous Colonel Wattenberg.

"Look, Colonel," said Daniel, in the tones of one bringing the news from Aix to Ghent, "Ruth is willing to sign at your terms. He's waiting at the Princess Martha right now. Right this very minute."

"I'm in no hurry," said Ruppert, who could be as autocratic as Bismarck when he chose, which was most of the time.

"Well, I am," answered Daniel, pulling out his watch like a condemned man waiting to hear from the governor's office. He then went tremolo and pulled out all the stops. On verbal bended knee, he told the Colonel all the frightening details, of his "exclusive," which threatened by the moment to become so exclusive that no one would touch it with a ten-foot pole. He told how he had out-silver-tongued the boy orator from the Platte to persuade Ruth to sign. And he mentioned the fact that the big fellow often got impatient standing around hotel lobbies, an argument which probably moved Ruppert more than any of Dan's poignant personal pleas.

With as much dispatch as was decorous, Daniel hustled Colonel Ruppert to the Princess Martha.

"Well, Root," said Ruppert, "you're ready to sign, hey?"

"Sure, Colonel," grinned the Babe, "where's that piece of paper?"

It developed that "the piece of paper," as Ruth so casually termed the contract which made him the highest salaried player in the history of baseball, wasn't available, but he and Ruppert shook hands and agreed to terms, Ruppert's terms.

"It was just 11:40 A.M. when they signed," Daniel always adds, as a sort of historical footnote. "My journalistic integrity, such as it was, was saved."

The formal signing took place a few days later, to the whirring accompaniment of newsreel cameras and the popping of flash bulbs. After the handshake, Ruth went out to Waterfront Park to help swell the gate for his friend, Judge Fuchs.

There always has been an unsolved mystery as to why the *Journal* never used Frick's story on Ruth's ultimatum. The accepted theory is that some time during the night, the Babe changed his mind about quitting and called Ford to inform him of his change of heart and that

Ford phoned the *Journal* desk instructing them to kill the story. And then forgot to phone Daniel.

"A natural oversight," agreed Dan. "After all, Ford didn't invite me to come into the Western Union office that night and look over his shoulder."

That was Ruth. He wanted, more than anything else, to play ball and to play ball he had to be under contract. That he was getting more money for playing ball than anybody has received before or since was part of Ruth's attractiveness to the non-fan. These sums stamped Babe as a man apart in his profession and was one reason for the tremendous adulation he received from people who weren't regular patrons of the

Press Association

The Babe thanks the huge crowd at Yankee Stadium on Babe Ruth Day, April 27, 1947. In the background, left to right: Ford Frick, National League president, friend and former ghost writer for Ruth; Mel Allen, radio announcer; Francis Cardinal Spellman, Archbishop of New York, and Commissioner A. B. Chandler.

ball parks and why people came to see Ruth play who never had been in a baseball stadium before—or since.

When the big fellow was cut again, it was the end of the trail. Financially, Ruth probably was paid commensurate with his ability to deliver, but when other ball players in the league began receiving as much, and more, than the Babe, he wasn't the big fellow any more.

It had, however, been fun while it lasted. Ruth had had a great ride, from the $600 contract he tremblingly signed with Jack Dunn to the one over which he and Colonel Ruppert shook hands for $80,000.

Ruth, mellowed with years and ravaged with illness, made an odd figure when he stood at home plate at Yankee Stadium on April 27, 1947, and listened to a thunderous ovation pour about his ears from nearly 60,000 fans, an ovation which was repeated in varying degrees in every ball park in the nation in observance of Babe Ruth Day.

He still had his camel's hair cap and his camel's hair coat, but his once black hair had grayed under X-ray treatments and his step was uncertain and halting as he made his way to home plate, the same home plate where he had made baseball history, in the park that his homers had built. His voice was curiously hoarse and weak, contrasted to the big, booming voice we all had known.

Ruth had listened to an invocation by His Eminence, Francis Cardinal Spellman, distinguished prelate of the Catholic Church, who at first was going to send a recording but came himself at Babe's personal request. He had heard praise from Commissioner Happy Chandler, from the two major league presidents, Will Harridge and Ford Frick, from a thirteen-year-old kid, Larry Cutler, of a junior American Legion team, from Mel Allen, the broadcaster of the Yankee games.

Then Ruth himself spoke into the microphone. Of all the speakers on this coast-to-coast broadcast, all except the youngster were more at home before a mike than he, but the big fellow was the only one who didn't read from a script. He spoke instead from his heart. In that strange voice, which was at once guttural and weak, Babe paid a plain and sincere tribute to the game of baseball. He said, among other things, that it was the greatest game there was. Babe said that baseball had been good to him.

That, Babe, was mutual.

11

The Big Scoop

Nobody who saw the hilarious and hectic 1934 World Series between the Tigers and the Gas House Gang of the Cardinals will ever forget it. And that goes double for those sports writers who covered it. As if the ebullient Dean brothers, Dizzy and Paul, weren't sufficiently fecund in producing copy, they were joined by their pappy for the Series. Everybody grants that the Deans were colorful performers. It may be added by one who knows—and so was their old man!

Despite the antics, and the pitching, of the Deans, Mickey Cochrane's Tigers were one up in the Series as we prepared to leave for the sixth and seventh games in Detroit. The elder Dean brother had been beaten 3 to 1 that Sunday afternoon at Sportsman's Park by one Tommy Bridges, a curve ball artist from Gordonsville, Tennessee.

There were three of us covering the Series for the New York *World-Telegram*—Joe Williams, the sports director and columnist, Dan Daniel, the baseball expert, and myself. Williams had decided to write his column about the then comparatively unknown Bridges, who had outpitched the Great Diz by an appreciable margin, and we were filling Joe in with background material on Tommy, stressing his mastery of the curve ball. (A curve ball which, it may be parenthetically observed, was good enough to permit Bridges to pitch a no-hitter in the Pacific Coast League some thirteen years later, when he was over forty years old.)

All this took place in Joe's compartment on the special train which was to take the writers to Detroit. After Williams had finished taking notes, we stepped out to the platform to get what we laughingly called "a mouthful of air" in the cavernous and smoke-filled Union Station of St. Louis. And along came Ruth.

The Babe, of course, covered all Series, in which he didn't play, for the Christy Walsh Syndicate. He chatted with the three of us for a couple of minutes and then Williams asked Babe a direct question, a question which had been puzzling all baseball for the past season and a question which the big fellow had consistently evaded.

"What are your plans, Babe?" asked Williams.

"Why, I'm going on that barnstorming trip to Japan," answered Ruth.

"No, I mean next year," said Joe impatiently. "With the Yankees. Are you going to play?"

Maybe the impatience of Williams communicated itself to Ruth; maybe he, too, was tired of ducking the issue.

"Not unless I'm manager," replied Babe. "Don't you think I'm entitled to the chance?"

Williams told Ruth that whether he thought Babe was entitled to a chance as manager didn't matter. It was what Ruppert and Barrow thought.

"Well," said Babe, preparing to move on, "I'm going to see the Colonel when I get back from Japan and have a showdown. And that's that."

Turned out it was, too.

Back the three of us scampered into Joe's drawing room. Williams looked at the notes he had taken on Bridges, crumpled them into a ball and tossed them to the floor. "It looks like the Babe has just shut out Mr. Bridges," he remarked.

Williams thereupon sat down and started to write the story of Ruth's decision not to play ball again under Joe McCarthy and to see Colonel Ruppert about the manager's job for himself when he returned from Japan. It made the first page, of course, and caused a sufficient sensation throughout the country to overshadow temporarily the World Series itself.

There was hell to pay in the press box at Navin Field before the teams started the sixth game. In telling Williams of his plans, Ruth had not only given Joe the best sports story of the year but had gone a little further and performed the acrobatic journalistic feat of scooping himself! For, remember, Babe was "covering" this Series himself. You can imagine the squawks which came from rival managing editors, who were shelling out hard cash for Ruth's by-line, when they found that a rival sheet had the banner yarn of the year, complete with direct quotes from their own private author.

The Hearst papers, practically all of which purchased Ruth's material from the Christy Walsh Syndicate, were in a particular dither at being sabotaged. There was strong pressure put upon the Babe to retract, to take refuge in that old political standby that he had been misquoted. Ruth, by now, realized he had committed some sort of a literary *faux pas* but refused to give ground. He didn't quite say, "I said it and I'm glad!" but he did admit that what Williams had written was what he had said.

Ruth, of course, had pulled a rock in divulging his intentions to Williams, or in making them public at all. He had tipped his mitt in advance and he knew that when the final showdown came with Ruppert and Barrow they would be well prepared for his ultimatum. He also knew, however, when he answered Williams' question that the answer was going to be printed.

It may have been that the big fellow was tired of the whole sham which existed between himself and McCarthy. During the season, going all the way back to a March broadcast by Walter Winchell during spring training, Babe and Joe had denied that there was any feud between them, but it was there all the time. In finally dragging it out in the open and in expressing his intentions, Ruth was forthright, if not diplomatic.

Ruth had had his eye on the manager's job of the Yankees ever since the death of Miller Huggins in September, 1929. He went to Ruppert then and asked for the job but the Colonel told him he would be more valuable to the Yanks as a player than as manager. As proof of where Ruth stood with the Yankee executives as a prospective manager, it is interesting to note that their first choice to succeed Huggins was Art Fletcher, the coach, but Fletch turned it down and Bob Shawkey was named. And when the Yanks limped home third under Shawkey in 1930, they turned to Joe McCarthy who had been let out in the final week of the season by the Cubs.

Wide World

Joe McCarthy wasn't too displeased when Babe took his talents elsewhere. Left to right: Lou Gehrig, Ford Frick, the Babe, Bill McKechnie and McCarthy, at Waterfront Park, St. Petersburg, March 17, 1935, after Ruth had joined the Braves.

McCarthy's release by the Cubs and his signing by the Yanks was not merely a happy combination of circumstances. Joe felt that he had received unjust criticism and interference from the late William Veeck, Cub president, as a result of the 1929 World Series. When the team was on its way to the Catalina training camp in the spring of 1930, Joe revealed to Warren Brown, Chicago sports writer, that he would not be with the Cubs after the end of the 1930 season, win, lose or draw.

Brown knew that Shawkey was no more than a stopgap manager for the Yankees and he saw Colonel Ruppert early in the 1930 season and told him the exact status of McCarthy with the Cubs. Ruppert, once he was convinced that William Wrigley, Chicago owner, would permit McCarthy to go, made plans to have him as manager in 1931, plans which included getting Bob Quinn, then with the Red Sox, to cede first call to McCarthy.

It was obvious from all these shenanigans that the Yankees never had any intention of hiring Ruth as manager at the ball park he had helped build. Ruppert had once told the Babe, "For years, Root, you haven't been able to take care of yourself. How can I turn my team over to you?"

This was near the close of the 1930 season when it was obvious that Shawkey was not going to be retained as manager. Ruth, of course, didn't know that Jake already had started negotiations to bring McCarthy to the Stadium and, although Babe protested that his wild oats had long since been sown and that he was now a happily married man, which in fact he was, it carried no weight with Ruppert. McCarthy was his choice.

Ruth was offered the Newark job later on, when he had become a problem child for McCarthy. By now the Babe had slowed down in the outfield almost to the point of being stationary and he wasn't hitting home runs as frequently. It was evident that Joe soon would have to make the decision which every manager dreads, to tell the star he can't play regularly any longer. And in McCarthy's case the decision would be doubly tough, because this was the greatest star of all and he antedated McCarthy with the ball club by more than a decade.

This was the basis of the Newark offer to Ruth. He was to go to the No. 1 farm of the Yankees and prove his managerial ability. He could still maintain his home in New York and be back in his Riverside Drive apartment every night when Newark played at home. The Babe turned it down, stating with simple dignity, "I've always been a big leaguer."

Christy Walsh, who had watched Ruth's affairs for him ever since 1921 and who, along with Ed Barrow, is responsible for Babe getting out of baseball with any money at all, has taken the blame for Babe's refusal to take the Newark job. He advised Babe to sit tight and that the Yankee job would eventually be his. While it is generous of Christy to take the blame, I doubt if Ruth would have accepted the Newark job even if Walsh had urged him to try his hand in the minors. Ruth's heart was set on managing in the majors, managing, to be specific, the Yankees.

There is no telling what might have been the outcome had Ruth gone to Newark. Although McCarthy was just as good a manager then as he ever was, which is to say pretty darn good, he wasn't held in the same high esteem which was to be his portion later. He had won one pennant with the Cubs, been routed in the World Series and, at the time the Newark job was offered to Ruth, hadn't distinguished himself with the Yankees. In fact some of the New York writers had hung the tag of "Second Place McCarthy" on him. The rash of pennants was to come later, with Joe DiMaggio.

When Ruth returned from the Orient, after traveling through Europe, his ship, the S.S. Manhattan, was met at Quarantine by a tugful of eager baseball writers. They wanted to know his plans. This was in January, 1935, some three months after the Babe had scooped himself by telling Joe Williams he would no longer play with the Yankees, unless he could be the manager.

The big fellow was vague. He said he had no immediate plans, except to go to the estate of a friend in Tuxedo Park, New York, and "shoot some peasants." One of the writers explained that he must have meant "pheasants" and Babe nodded his head and said, "I guess so—birds, anyway."

His baseball plans? Well, he didn't know. He supposed that one of these days "Barrows" would send him his contract and then it would be time enough to discuss what he was going to do in 1935.

The showdown, of course, came with the cards stacked in the Yankees' favor. With Babe now on the shady side of forty and growing no more nimble, he had become a hot potato. Waivers were asked on him in the American League and the Chicago White Sox claimed him. Ruppert got on the phone and explained to J. Louis Comiskey that the Babe would never be allowed to become the property of another American League club and would Mr. Comiskey please withdraw his claim so that the Colonel could make "other arrangements" for the Babe? Comiskey did and the "other arrangements" consisted of making Ruth a free agent and turning him over to Judge Emil Fuchs and the Boston Braves, a bizarre experience which will be dealt with in the next chapter.

The managerial job at Newark wasn't the only one Ruth missed. He also passed up a chance to manage the Detroit Tigers and also lost the offer of a manager's job with the Philadelphia Athletics. The Newark job Ruth refused, the Tiger decision he postponed until it was too late, but the chance for the Athletics job passed him by without his knowing it.

When Bucky Harris finished in the second division with Detroit in 1933 for the fifth straight time, Frank Navin decided that it was about time there were some changes made. He consulted with Barrow and Ruppert about the possibility of having Ruth manage the Tigers. The Babe had started to tail off in 1933, but he still batted over .300 and had power enough to hit thirty-four home runs. He also had hit a spectacular home run in the first major league All Star game that summer at Comiskey Park.

The deal had reached the point where the Yankees were willing to give up Ruth, and Barrow had his eye on an outfielder the Tigers were to give in exchange. Navin wished to see Ruth in Detroit for a personal interview before closing the deal. There were many details to go into, not the least of which was his contract. Babe strangely replied that he couldn't see him, that he was leaving for San Francisco to take a ship to Hawaii for an exhibition series.

When Barrow learned that Ruth had declined Navin's telegraphed invitation for an interview, he called up the Babe. Ed foresaw the contractual amputation job which would have to be done on the big fellow if he were still with the Yankees by the following spring and was all for Babe going to Detroit as manager. It would get the ball club off the spot and it would give Ruth the opportunity he had been seeking ever since the death of Miller Huggins.

"Aren't you going to stop off in Detroit and see Mr. Navin, Babe?" asked Barrow.

"No," said Babe carelessly, "I'll see him when I get back from Honolulu."

"Well, Babe," was Barrow's final admonition, "suit yourself, but remember that job won't stay open forever."

It didn't, either. Whether Navin decided that a person who would pass up a chance to manage so carelessly was too irresponsible to be a manager or whether he was personally piqued at Babe's lofty postponement will never be known. When Ruth returned from the Islands and called Mr. Navin, he was told that the appointment had gone to Mickey Cochrane.

Ruth sailed into the Pacific once more, this time after the 1934

Keystone

In Japan, Ruth was king. Here he poses with a group of Japanese bat boys at Koshien Stadium, Osaka, in November, 1934.

Series, during which he had perpetrated the well-nigh incredible feat of scooping himself. He toured the Orient with an All-American League team led by Connie Mack and he made an impression in Japan which was erased only when the B-29's came over with fire bombs. Although the Babe by now was almost as round at the girth as one of the Son of Heaven's own imperial wrestlers, he still had enough power of arm and quickness of eye to be partial to Japanese pitching. He whaled home runs all over the land of the Rising Sun, since set, and had a better than .400 average for the tour.

At the time of this trip Mack was seventy-two and was thinking of retiring, a thought which doesn't seem to have occurred to him seriously since. It struck Connie that Ruth might be a happy choice as manager. Mack knew Ruth, of course, since the big fellow had come into the American League and knew that there were a lot of managerial qualifications in which the Babe was, to put it charitably, somewhat short of perfection. On the other hand, he knew that Ruth had an undeniable talent for the game and believed that with Babe as part-time player, pinch-hitter and manager the Athletics would be strengthened. It was Mack's intention to leave the bench and retire to the front office as an executive, giving Ruth the benefit of his experience in player deals and so on, but allowing the Babe to run the club from the bench.

It is probable that Mack also figured Ruth would serve to entice some additional customers through the turnstiles at Shibe Park during the years to come. Connie had sold the key men of his championship teams of 1929-30-31 and the A's that season had slipped into the second division. The last time he had broken up a championship team by selling its stars, the Athletics had remained in the cellar for a decade, and the thought probably occurred to Connie that were history to repeat itself, Ruth would be a handy guy to have around.

Ruth was entirely ignorant of the designs Mack had upon him. What would have been his reactions it is hard to say. The Babe was having his own personal troubles. His family was feuding with the Gehrigs and it upset the big fellow. He never did know how to handle a feud, for his idea of trouble was to have a blow-up and get it over with. Smoldering anger was an alien thing to a man whose emotions were always close to the surface.

One of the other ball players on the tour was acting the gallant by walking Miss Julia Ruth, the Babe's adopted daughter, around the deck as the Empress of Britain plowed her majestic way through the Pacific from Honolulu to Yokohama. He happened to espy a familiar figure reading in a deck chair and prepared to halt alongside Lou Gehrig.

"Don't stop," whispered young Julia, "the Ruths don't speak to the Gehrigs.'

"On shipboard, they do," replied this punctilious ball player. "You don't snub people at sea."

The incident is mentioned here only to reveal how high the feelings were running between the feudists. It was an unhappy experience for Babe, who had wanted no part of it in the first place. He was to prove that within five years when he threw his arms around Lou at Yankee Stadium on Gehrig Day and sobbed unrestrainedly and unashamedly.

Nevertheless, the feud was there and it spread on shipboard like smallpox. The tourists were being split into two factions. Connie

Press Association

Ruth throws his arm around his old side-kick at Lou Gehrig Appreciation Day, Yankee Stadium, July 4, 1939.

noted it, for all of his aloofness from the ball players, and promptly changed his mind about Babe Ruth as a manager. He decided, rightly or wrongly, that Mrs. Ruth had too much influence over the slugger.

"I couldn't have made Babe manager," he told Joe Williams the following spring at the A's training base in Fort Meyers, Florida. "His wife would have been running the club in a month."

One of the most oft-repeated phrases concerning Ruth's baseball sense was, "I never saw him throw to the wrong base." Who first coined it there is no way of telling, but it was in popular use about the Babe as long ago as 1923. It was uttered by other ball players, by umpires, by baseball writers and baseball officials.

It was, of course, intended as a compliment, but on close examination, it doesn't stand up very well. To begin with, how many chances does an outfielder get to throw to the wrong base in the course of a season? And, to avoid throwing to the wrong base, there is only one cardinal rule to keep in mind, which is to throw ahead of the runner. Check back in your own experience and recall how many wrong throws you have seen an outfielder make, how many times a base runner has taken an extra base because the outfielder failed to make the orthodox throw. You'll find it mounts up to very few over a six-month season.

While the most reiterated accolade tossed to the Babe's baseball acumen was, in effect, damning him with faint praise, or, as the late Percy Hammond once put it, praising him with faint damns, there is no question that Ruth had an instinctive flair for the game. He proved this hundreds of times by bunting when the opposition expected him to pull for the fence, by hitting to the opposite field to prevent overshifting against him and, in his younger days, daringly trying for the extra base.

Ruth was a good base runner until his tonnage caught up with him. He often stole better than ten a season, twice getting as many as seventeen, and stealing bases calls for more than speed alone. A successful base stealer must be a good observer; he must know when to break on a pitcher. All this the big fellow could do.

Signs, however, remained a black art to the Babe. That mysterious phase of baseball whereby a coach touches his hand to his ear, to the insignia on his uniform, to the peak of his cap, etc., to inform the

Keystone

Ty Cobb, who had his chance to manage, and Babe, who never did get his chance, talk things over at a Stadium opener after Ty joined the Philadelphia Athletics.

batter that he is to take or hit at the next pitch never made any impression on Ruth. Whatever he may have done with the Red Sox as a young fellow, Babe never took or gave a sign in all of his fifteen seasons with the Yankees. It wasn't the handicap it might seem. There was no sense in picking out a ball for him to hit, because Babe had better eyes for that than any one who ever played. And there was no need for Ruth to signal ahead to the base runner that he was going to put on the hit-and-run, because when Babe hit the runner rarely needed a headstart.

Few top-flight baseball stars have made good managers. Ty Cobb never was a good manager and neither was Rogers Hornsby. Tris Speaker won a pennant and a World's Championship with Cleveland but otherwise failed to distinguish himself. Christy Mathewson, a master pitcher and master craftsman on the pitching mound, was a failure as a manager. So was Walter Johnson. The theory advanced in these cases is that the stars are inclined to be too impatient with the material at hand. Their own playing standards were so high, and their skill so natural, that they couldn't see why those under them didn't learn quickly. This, of course, is only a theory. Your most successful managers are usually men who were merely run-of-the-mill players in their active careers, men like Joe McCarthy, who never did make the majors, or Bill McKechnie who finally hit .321 at Minneapolis after fifteen years of trying.

On that score the evidence is against Ruth because baseball came as natural as sleeping to him. Since patience was never one of his virtues it is hard to picture Babe as a developer of young ball players, although he may have been able to help many hitters. Ruth had a good personality and players liked him. That, of course, was when Babe was playing. What his disposition might have been as a manager there is no way of telling.

Any time Ruth ever talked baseball, which wasn't as often as you might think, his observations were sound. Quite a few times I discovered Babe to be surprisingly accurate in his estimates of various young players, even though Ruth's appraisal of them was at direct variance with the majority opinion.

One thing Ruth had, and one thing which would have helped as a manager had he ever been granted the opportunity, was that he was a grand competitor. That part of Babe's make-up has been stressed surprisingly little in any account of his career, but he was a bear-down guy from away back. He took almost foolhardy chances on fly balls merely because he wanted to win.

All this, of course, is academic. Ruth never did get the chance to manage and for a variety of reasons. He turned down one job flat, passed up another through carelessness and was counted out on a third without even knowing he was being considered. It is on record, however, that he was passed up three times for the one managerial job he wanted, piloting his own Yankees. And he was passed up by those who knew him best.

To close this chapter on Ruth's managerial aspirations, mention must be made of a qualification he laid before Colonel Ruppert in one of his bids for the stewardship of the Yankees. The Babe told Jake he would make an ideal manager because he knew all the answers.

"Colonel, I've been through the ropes," Ruth is supposed to have said. "I can point out the pitfalls to the younger players and tell them what to avoid."

It is rather difficult to conceive of the Babe resorting to such high-flown rhetoric to describe his early journeys along the primrose paths. But in all justice to the big fellow, it must be recorded that he did know all about the pitfalls which yawned before a ball player. He had, in fact, scouted most of them himself.

12

The Tinsel Tarnishes

Bill Corum, standard bearer for the Hearst legions which had been scooped during the 1934 World Series when Babe Ruth had bared his soul, and his ambitions, to Joe Williams, had his revenge a little over four months later. In his column in the New York *Journal-American* in late February, 1935, Corum was able to announce that the Yankees were releasing Ruth and that he was to become the manager of the Boston Braves. This was big news, bigger even than Williams' October scoop because, where that dealt with something which was to be done, Corum was announcing a *fait accompli.* The Yankee office confirmed the story within twenty-four hours.

To say that New York's baseball fans were shocked would be a slight exaggeration. "Surprised" is the better term. After Ruth's World Series blast against Joe McCarthy they half-expected to see the big fellow go elsewhere. On the other hand, Babe had trouble before and it had been patched up. In fifteen years the fans of New York had become used to the vagaries of Ruth, used to seeing him and used to reading about him. Whatever shock there was lay in the fact that Ruth would do his ball playing elsewhere in the future.

The attitude New York took toward the announcement was perhaps best summed up by John Kieran in his daily sports column in the New York *Times* for February 27, 1935. Those who know John only for his amazing memory and astounding erudition on the radio program, Information Please, may not realize that he once was one of the country's better sports writers, a gifted writer and an extremely accurate reporter. His column, describing the announcement of Babe's release was headed "THIS WAY TO BOSTON" and read as follows:

> Well, he's gone. Fifteen years in a Yankee uniform and now back to Boston again. But it's a fine solution and a perfect answer to the old query: "If you don't like it around here, why don't you go back where you came from?"
>
> There were three men in blue suits, blue shirts and blue ties in the big office in the big brewery. From left to right they were Babe Ruth, Judge Fuchs and Colonel Ruppert. It will be noted that Judge Fuchs was the man in the middle. It was a dark day outside, fitting weather

Wide World

The Three Men in Blue—Judge Emil Fuchs, Ruth and Colonel Jake Ruppert, with Babe, appropriately enough, in the middle—at Ruppert's Brewery, February 26, 1935, when Babe's contract was assigned to the Braves.

for what was a sad occasion in New York. The wind was wailing and the skies were weeping.

Colonel Ruppert adjusted his horn-rimmed glasses, made a little speech and handed the Babe a white slip that was, in effect, a one-way ticket to Boston. But technically it was a document reading:

"Feb. 26, 1935.

"Mr. George H. Ruth:

"You are hereby notified as follows:

"1. That you are unconditionally released."

It bore the corporate seal of the Yankee club and was signed by Jacob Ruppert, president.

The Colonel made a kindly little speech in which he kept referring to the Babe as "Ruth," this being a habit with the Yankee owner. Every one else calls him the Babe, *comme-ça,* but the Colonel is different.

In bidding good-by to his former henchman Colonel Ruppert said that he and Ruth had gotten along well for many years. They had their little differences from time to time, but Ruth had told him once that he considered him (Colonel Ruppert) his second father and—

"I shoulda said Santa Claus," interrupted the Babe.

The Colonel smiled a sad smile and went on to say that this was an opportunity for Ruth to better himself and he wouldn't stand in his way. On the contrary, he wished him every success in his new venture, and the same to Judge Fuchs. Copies of the exchange of letters on the whole affair were there and the bystanders could read them and see how, why and when the whole thing was arranged. That was all he had to say.

The Babe was next at bat. He was standing there with his arms folded over his ample chest and the first thing he said was "Ha-hum!" in a loud voice.

This was well received, but his audience craved more, so the Babe put both hands in his side pockets, advanced his right foot and went on to say that he had enjoyed playing with the Yankees very much and he never had any trouble with the Colonel. Everything was fine, but he couldn't play any more as a regular and here was a chance that "Mister" Fuchs was offering him—the Babe called him "Mister Fuchs"; every one else calls him "Judge"; the three men in blue really should get better acquainted.

Then the Babe said that he had always given his best to the Yankees and he meant to say that he would do the same for the Braves, but he got his signs mixed somewhere in the tenseness of the situation and said "against the Braves" instead of "for the Braves," whereupon Judge Fuchs looked at him in astonishment, took out a handkerchief and wiped his brow.

The Babe said that that was about all he could say and then someone asked him what his duties would be as vice president of the Braves.

That caught the Babe off base a bit and he got as far as "Why— hugh— I— er" when Judge Fuchs cut in with:

"Advisory capacity; be consulted on club deals and so forth."

"A vice president," said Colonel Ruppert. "Why, a vice president signs checks. Everybody knows that."

"That's right," said Judge Fuchs with a grin, "I'll give him a check right now if he'll sign it."

Then Judge Fuchs, the third of the blue-uniformed principals, made his little speech and was getting along nobly when Colonel Ruppert cut in with:

"Pardon me, Judge, but I forgot to say—and you and Ruth can testify to it—that Boston is getting Ruth and Ruth is getting what he wants and I'm getting nothing. Not a cent. I wouldn't stand in Ruth's way and I'm glad to help Judge Fuchs and baseball, so I'm giving Ruth his unconditional release. I don't get a cent out of it."

The Babe nodded and Judge Fuchs raised his right hand solemnly and bore witness to the truth of the Colonel's sad statement. There are the facts and Colonel Ruppert really was parting with a chattel of value in this free-handed way, but the bystanders consoled themselves with the thought that the good Colonel had something left and would not, even after giving away the Babe, go limping over the hill to the poorhouse.

Judge Fuchs then completed his speech and after that the bystanders started to ask questions. Would Ruth draw as much from the Braves this year as he drew from the Yankees?

"I think he will," said Judge Fuchs, and then added, "How much did he get last year?" Somebody said $35,000, causing Judge Fuchs to pull out his handkerchief and wipe his brow again. He looked at the ceiling, thought a moment and then went on: "Yes, I hope he will—and more."

The point is that the Babe is going to get a salary and a share of the profits of the club if there are any profits. There's where the Babe can help himself by making some profits for himself. It's a big job and that's why the Judge went after the big fellow to do it.

There were more questions as to what Bill McKechnie would say or do and when the Yankees had decided to let Ruth go and who called up whom on the phone and how many games the Babe would play and in what position. The three men in blue said that all the questions were answered in the letters, copies of which were offered in abundance, and there was nothing more to be said at the moment. Then they had to go into another room to be photographed and they marched through the door, three stout men in blue. The Babe was the tallest, the Judge was the stoutest and the Colonel was by all odds the bluest.

Ruth's return to the scene of his early triumphs should have been felicitous. The Babe was far better known in Boston than he was in New York for Babe had been around, about and on the town as a youngster in Boston, whereas in New York the big fellow stayed under cover when he wasn't at the ball park. Kids growing up in Boston had billboards pointed out to them, billboards through which the Babe had driven his speeding roadster in a moment of exhilaration, or "silent policemen," those concrete traffic warnings, upon which Ruth's car had descended with a grinding of fenders. New York has no such monuments to Ruth's early craving for speed, although he did once turn over an Auburn car in an alley behind the Concourse Plaza Hotel in the Bronx. On the very day it had been presented to him, too.

Despite the warmer, personal feeling Bostonians should have entertained for the Babe, his brief stay with the Braves was not a happy one. On May 25, he collected three home runs against the Pirates in Forbes Field but a few days later, playing at Redland Field, Cincinnati, the

Keystone

Although Babe was far from a model driver, he was willing to lend his name and presence to official safety drives, such as the one pictured above.

Babe virtually finished his major league career. He was struck out three times by Si Johnson and in going up the left field embankment after a batted ball, he pulled some muscles in his leg. He stuck it out for a while and quit abruptly in the middle of the next inning.

As Ruth limped from his position in left to the runway by the home club's dugout leading to the clubhouse, most of those in the press box thought they were seeing the last appearance of the big fellow as a major leaguer. It wasn't quite that, for a couple of days later he played on Decoration Day in Philadelphia without in any way distinguishing himself or adding to his record.

The Giants played in Boston the next day, May 31, and Babe was on the Braves' bench, in civilian clothes, wearing a Braves' windbreaker with a Turkish towel swathed around his neck. He had a heavy cold, he explained, but there was something in the air that indicated all was not smooth sailing between the Babe and his employers.

It wasn't until two days later, Sunday, June 2, that the big blowoff came. The press box in Braves Field is unofficially known as "Earache Alley" because of the garrulity of its occupants, both native and imported. There was a moment's quiet during the game between the Giants and Braves when press handouts were distributed among the Boston writers, the gist of which seemed to be that Judge Fuchs was yielding control of the Braves to what was rather euphemistically described as "a group of New England sportsmen" but which sounded suspiciously like the Judge's creditors.

For some reason this statement was distributed to the Boston writers only, although they willingly shared their intelligence with the visiting firemen from New York. It looked as if sectionalism had indeed reared its ugly head when a messenger came up from the bowels of Braves Field with the startling information that: "Babe Ruth would like to see the New York writers in the Braves' clubhouse after the game."

The Boston writers meanwhile were trying to digest the information furnished them by their own couriers but availed themselves of the invitation extended to them by their New York brethren to come along with them and make it open house in the Boston dressing room.

"I'm quitting," said Ruth, as simply as that.

Perhaps the most peculiar thing about this stark announcement which meant the end of the active playing career of the greatest player

Keystone

The alpha and omega of Babe's career in Boston—breaking in as a kid southpaw with the Red Sox in 1914 and bowing out as a paunchy slugger with the Braves in 1935.

the game had ever seen was that nobody seemed surprised. That and the fact that Rabbit Maranville, who had just returned to the game after a fifteen-month layoff as the result of a broken leg sustained in an exhibition game against the Yankees in St. Petersburg, was stomping around the clubhouse, demanding to know who in *the* hell was the official scorer who had given him an error on a ground ball which had taken a bad hop and damn near broke his breastbone.

If nobody seemed terribly surprised at the big fellow's announcement, I must also report that nobody seemed greatly concerned. There was a sullenness about the clubhouse that was difficult to describe. Aside from Rabbit's bleating about the unjust error with which he had been charged, there was no outward manifestation of animosity, but it was there just the same. It was as if Babe and the rest of the ball club were worlds apart.

Bill McKechnie, the manager of the Braves, who probably was more embarrassed than anyone in the room, as he figured to be because of the ambiguity of the multitudinous titles of the Babe—vice president, left fielder and assistant manager—brought over a box of baseballs for the Babe to autograph for him. I asked Bill point blank if there had been any trouble between him and Ruth and he answsered: "No, everything is and has been fine." Which of course it wasn't and never had been.

When Babe was asked what had prompted him to chuck up the sponge, he gave the most implausible reason of a career which had almost as many records in the implausible reasons division as it had in home runs.

"Judge Fuchs won't let me go down to see the Normandie," was the astounding answer. He then went on to explain that the Normandie, pride of the French Line, was to reach New York on its maiden voyage during the following week, and he had been invited to attend the reception aboard the new luxury liner after it had docked. And the Braves were playing a game that day and he wasn't going to be excused from classes by Judge Fuchs.

There was, of course, more to it than that. The profits that John Kieran wrote about and in which Babe expected to share weren't there. Furthermore, Ruth had expected to be given some guarantee about his elevation from his nebulous title of "assistant manager" to something more substantial, such as the managership itself. This apparently had been promised to him, either actually or tacitly, although never in writing.

From the Braves' dressing room the writers trooped to the Fuchs' office. The Judge received them warmly, even though his ball club was slowly sliding out from under him on a flood tide of I.O.U.'s. He was inclined to deprecate Ruth's resignation as a minor matter, which it probably was to him at that harried moment. Somebody asked if Ruth hadn't made a lot of money for the Braves in their exhibition games and somebody (not Fuchs) replied that the Braves "always drew well in the spring."

The Judge was asked if the Babe was going to be paid in full for the season, get his ten-days' pay or what adjustment would be made.

"Mr. Ruth will get what is coming to him," equivocated the Judge. And to this day nobody knows whether it was a promise or a threat.

On Monday, the Babe and Mrs. Ruth threw their luggage in the back of their car and motored to New York. They couldn't have been

Keystone

Two great American League stars, members of the Hall of Fame, whose active careers ended in the National League with the Boston Braves—Babe Ruth and George Sisler.

much beyond the city limits of Boston when McKechnie delivered an invective against the big fellow, to the effect that he had been a disturbing and disharmonious influence on the club and that the Braves would be better off without him. For the records, it must be noted that the Braves lost 115 games that season and that *is* a record. They were rained out of one game, too.

Baseball is a game of many contrasts and nowhere is the change more startling than in the difference between an opening game and the last one of the season. Opening day is a gala affair, with the lively, hopeful air of a christening about it. Closing day can be likened to nothing so much as a wake, swathed as it is in an air of melancholia. Between Game No. 1 and Game No. 154, many sunny hopes have turned to ashes, many bright dreams have turned to nightmares.

It is unlikely that the contrast ever was brought home more sharply than it was in the season of 1935. I saw Ruth open the season at Braves Field in Boston, on a murky, chilly day, with a marrow-biting wind blowing in from Buzzard's Bay and the hint of a blizzard in the air. The spirit in the stands, however, contained all the sunshine which the day itself lacked, for the prodigal had come home to roost.

Many were the fatted calves killed in his honor. Governors of a half dozen New England States and a sprinkling of mayors were on hand to honor the great man. Newsreel cameras whirred and flash bulbs popped. The press box was jammed to the gunwales with writers from all over the East and 20,000 shivering faithful in the stands applauded joyfully as the Babe did his stuff, smiting Carl Hubbell for a home run which enabled the Braves to rise in triumph over the Giants.

Ruth closed out that 1935 season at Dyckman Oval in the Bronx, playing with a pick-up team of semi-pros against the New York Cubans. The weather, for late September, was mellower and milder by far than it had been back in Braves Field that April afternoon, but the stands were somber. The spectators seemed to sense that they were sitting in on something pathetic, almost as if they had come across John McCormack acting as a singer waiter in a beer joint. There were about 8,000 present, an overflow crowd and the biggest in the history of Dyckman Oval. There were neither newsreel nor still cameras in evidence and no telegraph keys clattered brassily in the press box, which had less than a half-dozen occupants. No civic dignitaries, not even an alderman, could be observed in the crowd.

On opening day in Boston, Ruth's home run against Hubbell was the shot heard 'round the baseball world. He hit a two-bagger on closing day against a sepia southpaw, one Lefty Louis Tiant, called "Cuba's Hubbell." He walked once and sent two towering flies to an ebony-hued right fielder named Spearman, who is called the "Brown Lloyd Waner," which is giving Spearman several shades the best of it.

When the first game of the double header, and the only one in which Ruth was advertised to appear, was concluded, the Babe, feeling perhaps that the fans who had paid $1.10 for grandstand seats and 55 cents for the bleachers hadn't a complete run for their money, staged an extra-curricular exhibition of hitting.

Batting against Clyde Barfoot, who had been briefly with Pittsburgh in his younger days, Ruth stayed at the plate for five minutes and belted a half-dozen homers, four of which landed on the roof of a garage behind the right field fence, some 400 feet away. His last drive screamed 500 feet to dead center and then the big fellow dashed to his car, fighting his way through autograph seekers. He was sweaty, dirty, tired and happy—happier by far than he had been that June afternoon when I heard him forswear baseball forever in the Braves' clubhouse at Boston.

History was made at Ebbets Field on the night of June 15, 1938. It was the first time a major league game had been played at night in Brooklyn and, in the course of that game, Johnny Vander Meer, pitching for the Cincinnati Reds, pitched no-hit, no-run ball against the Dodgers, thus becoming the first pitcher in all the annals of baseball to pitch two successive no-hit, no-run games. He had previously pitched a no-hit, no-run game against Boston in Cincinnati on June 11.

Brooklyn fans had a full twenty-four hours in which to digest the twin wonders of Larry MacPhail's arc lights and Vander Meer's double-no-hitter, since it was the custom in those more leisurely times to give ball clubs a day off after they had played a night game. When the Dodgers returned to the wars again at Ebbets Field, against these same Reds, they lost a double header in broad daylight.

MacPhail decided it was high time something was done about this deplorable state of affairs, a decision the Brooklyn fans had reached some hours in advance of him. He decided to hire Babe Ruth as coach. It was believed this extraordinary announcement would serve to take the minds of the clients from the athletes they were being forced to gaze upon. Manager Burleigh Grimes already had a couple of coaches, but none of them had shown any marked ability to drag fans through the turnstiles, although they were considered able men in their own profession.

It was decided that Ruth should coach at first base and, as his contribution to the drive to lift the Dodgers by their collective bootstraps, he would give the signs to right-handed batters. Ruth and his manager, Christy Walsh, met with MacPhail and a contract was signed giving Babe $15,000 for the remainder of the season.

Ruth was unveiled in Flatbush on a Sunday afternoon and it was soon evident that in assigning Babe to give the signs from first base a

Wide World

The Babe is in the middle again. Ruth with Manager Burleigh Grimes (left) and Captain Leo Durocher, as he joined the Dodgers as a coach, June 19, 1938.

grievous error had been made. The first Dodger batsman was a left-handed hitter, so Babe had a brief respite, but the next was Ki-Ki Cuyler, a right-hander. Ruth so gummed up the signs that he confused not only himself but Cuyler as well and the entire project was abandoned instanter and forthwith. The big fellow never gave another sign as long as he was with the Dodgers and contented himself at first base merely by assuming the duties of a traffic cop.

If Ruth was of no strategic value to the Dodgers, he was far from a financial drag. Fans came out just to look at the great man, when they wouldn't possibly have come out to look at the Dodgers. Furthermore, exhibition games suddenly appeared on the Brooklyn schedule where none had been before. These exhibition games, eight or ten of them, grossed $14,000 which almost paid the Babe's salary right there.

Playing first base in these exhibition games, Ruth literally took his life in hand when he went to bat against wild, young, strong-armed pitchers, all eager to have the distinction of striking out the home run champion. By then Babe's once famed batting sight had been badly dimmed and he could scarcely see at all out of one eye without glasses. All the games were at night and in many of the parks in the smaller towns the lighting system wasn't as bright as the one you have in your hall closet. It was miraculous that he was never hit. With all these disadvantages, the big fellow managed to hit one home run, a belt in a game in Albany against a young farm hand of the Cincinnati Reds, a prodigious poke which, in the parlance of the players, Babe "hit nine miles."

Oddly enough this wasn't exactly exploitation of Ruth, for in the first exhibition game, which was played at Newark, the old war horse phoned road secretary John McDonald the afternoon of the game and said, "I'm ready to play a couple of innings tonight if you think it will help the gate." It would and it did.

This was in MacPhail's first year in Brooklyn and the Dodgers were in sorry shape. It was an open secret that Burleigh Grimes would be through after the season and the manager's job was up for grabs. You could sense the ball club being split into two factions. Ruth, as ever, had managerial ambitions and the same lofty aspirations were stirring in the breast of Leo Durocher, who was then merely the shortstop of a seventh-place ball club.

There was nothing subtle about Durocher. He made no bones

about his goal and he doubtless regarded Ruth as an intruder when the Babe was made a coach in mid-June. He was outspoken about the Babe's lack of finesse as a coach and it flared into open warfare one day in the Polo Grounds before a game with the Giants. A fistfight was prevented only by the intervention of the other players in the Dodger locker room.

It seems that the Dodgers had won a game a few days before, which was surprising enough, but even more surprising was that it had been won through the skillful manipulation of a hit-and-run play. One of the younger writers traveling with the Dodgers credited Ruth with giving the sign for the game-winning strategem.

Durocher was openly critical of Ruth in the clubhouse that day. He wanted to know where Babe got off to tell anybody that he had given the hit-and-run sign and told Ruth that he lacked the brains to give a sign. Babe might have lost his eye at the plate but he had lost none of his old invective and he came back red hot at Leo. The two charged each other. Some witnesses say that Durocher managed to land a punch on Ruth's chest, others that they were separated before even this single reported blow was landed.

There has been a story current time and again and printed once or twice that Durocher told the Babe off when both were with the Yankees. Leo is supposed to have remarked that all Ruth had was a strong back while he (Leo) had a brain and would be in baseball long after the big fellow had faded from the picture. This I doubt, not because Durocher wouldn't have the spunk to challenge Ruth, or anybody else, but because there was no greater coolness between Durocher and Ruth in the Lip's two years with the Yankees than there was between Leo and the rest of the ball club. Durocher may very well have made the remark attributed to him, because Leo was always making remarks, but there never was an outward sign of a lasting feud between the two.

When Durocher succeeded Grimes to the managership of the Dodgers in November, 1935, it marked the end of Ruth's last connection with organized baseball. MacPhail made no effort to bring him back in 1939 as coach, because he knew Leo wouldn't accept him as such. And it is extremely doubtful that Larry could have lured the Babe back for another season, for the big fellow probably was no more anxious to serve under Durocher than Durocher was to have him.

Once more Ruth felt that he had been let down and exploited. Again the big fellow was bitter, a condition which was becoming chronic with him. To the Babe's way of reckoning he had been passed by once too often for a manager's shot, by the Yankees, the Braves and the Dodgers, to say nothing of the Tigers and Athletics. He was seen less frequently around Yankee Stadium or any ball park.

It was the kids, Ruth's old standbys, who brought him back to the ball parks. He appeared at a promotional game or two for *Esquire* magazine and found himself knee-deep in male bobby soxers. The Babe was almost childishly pleased at this evidence of affection and esteem from the youngsters. The vast majority of the letters which poured in on him during his eighty-two-day siege at French Hospital were from kids. And when Ruth left the hospital, broken in health, he accepted a post from the Ford Motor Company to promote juvenile baseball, to serve as a consultant in that company's American Legion junior baseball program.

"I'll do as much for the kids as my health will permit," he said in accepting the position.

After all, this bond between Ruth and the kids is not so terribly strange that it passeth all understanding. For the big fellow, you see, was never anything but a kid himself.